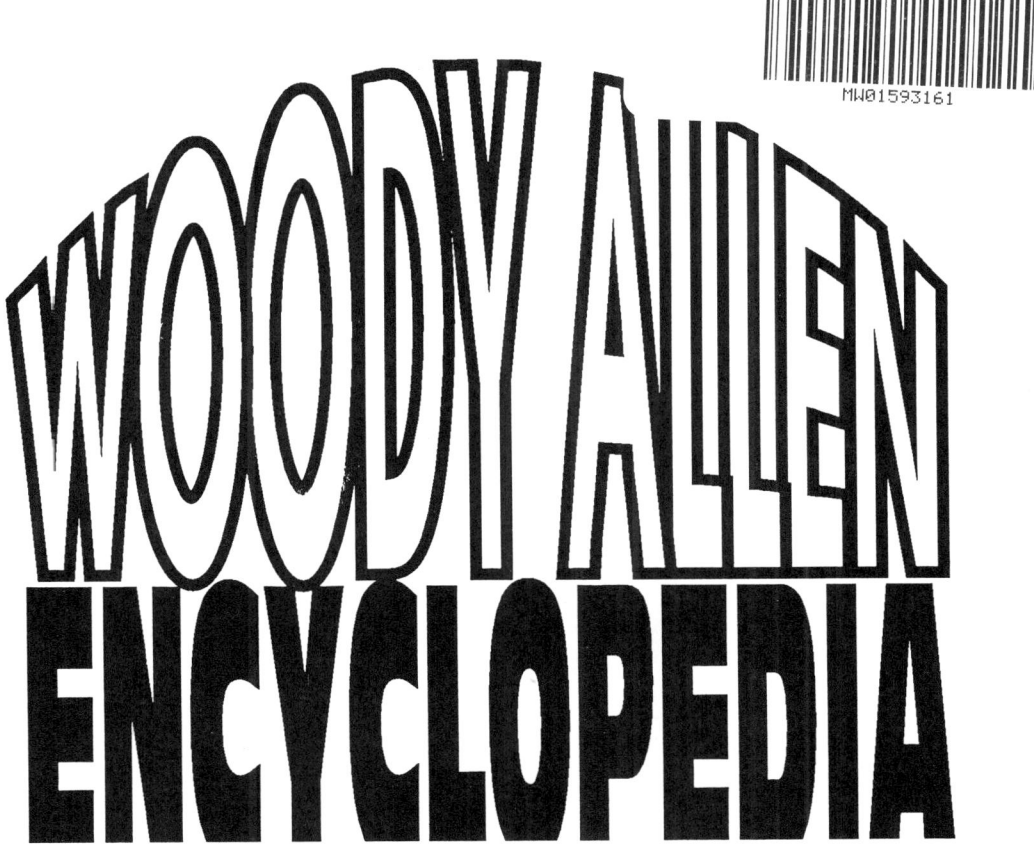

WOODY ALLEN ENCYCLOPEDIA

Almost Everything You Wanted To Know About the Woodster But Were Afraid To Ask (* And Alot Of Things You Didn't Want To Know But We'll Tell You Anyway)

By Mark A. Altman
With Additional Material From
David Ian Salter, Mitchell Rubinstein, Thomas Doherty And Diane Eisenberg

Books for the entertainment buyer

PIONEER

Designed and Edited by Hal Schuster
with assistance from David Lessnick

Dedicated to Woody Allen, the man whose given us all so much laughter and joy. Lighten up and thanks for the Matzoh, er, Manhattan. Now if you were only an urban planner.

Library of Congress Cataloging-in-Publication Data
Mark A. Altman—
THE WOODY ALLEN ENCYCLOPEDIA

1. THE WOODY ALLEN ENCYCLOPEDIA (popular culture)
I. Title

Published by Pioneer Books, Inc., 5715 N. Balsam Rd., Las Vegas, NV, 89130.

First Printing, 1990

I would like to graciously acknowledge the many individuals who made this book possible including my co-authors David Ian Salter (a Brandeis graduate who knows nothing about Adolph Loos), Mitchell Rubinstein (a dental student whose is also a Brandeis graduate who knows absolutely nothing about Adolph Loos) and Diane Eisenberg (yet another Brandeis graduate who may or may not know about Adolph Loos. I don't know, I'll have to ask her oneday. I know she definitely hasn't been to any socialist summer camps). Special thanks to Brandeis Professor Thomas Doherty for allowing me to reprint his two intriguing anaylses of PURPLE ROSE & ALICE (and for being one of the few Professor's who thought of art and not popcorn when teaching film at Brandeis). Not only does he know who Adolph Loos is, but could probably right a book about him. I couldn't have pulled it off without you guys.

Special thanks to publisher Hal Schuster who tolerated my move to California and its resulting series of mini-calamities. Only an idiot like me would use STAR TREK movers becasue of the name.

Illa Dhalla, for going to see ALICE with me, who forever proved to me that beautiful models don't have to be stupid also. To a classy, intelligent and wonderful woman, may we see many more Woody Allen movies together.

For their cheerleading from the sidelines; my buddy Steven Simak who I don't think has ever seen a Woody Allen movie — sorry about all the matzo ball jokes, Bob Posin and his incredible wife Bano Gilani (let's NEVER go to Michael's Pub again - Woody's great, the price and the service stinks! I'm still paying off that second mortgage to pay for the dinner), my favorite brother Ira — because I forgot to thank him in the last book and he certainly deserves to be thanked, my father for forgetting to tell Tony Roberts I was working on a book about Woody Allen when he met him at Gracey Mansion (TYPICAL!) and for getting through his bout with pnemonia with flying colors (and for the hysterical Dr. Kenneth Weiner for helping him with that, I'm sure he's seen a few Woody Allen movies) and my absolutely fantastic and supportive mother Gail I. Altman-Orenstein (boy, that's a mouthful) who once again would constantly call me to tell me to work on my writing except when I tried to hang up when she would ask me what's my rush. She still doesn't think I can write.

Of course, any acknowldgement in a Woody Allen book would not be complete without a warm and loving nod to my (adjectives cannot describe) grandmother Rebecca without whom I could never appreciate the incredibly wonderful and telling Jewish humor of Woody Allen. My grandmother who makes Mae Questel in NEW YORK STORIES look tame in comparison. Everyone should have a grandmother like her.

MARK A. ALTMAN is a promient film and television journalist whose work has appeared in such magazines as PANACHE, STARLOG, COMICSCENE, SCIENCE-FICTION VIDEO MAGAZINE and CINEFANTASTIQUE which featured his acclaimed cover stories on LICENSE TO KILL and STAR TREK: THE NEXT GENERATION. He is the author of the bestselling TWIN PEAKS: AN UNOFFICIAL VISITORS GUIDE TO TWIN PEAKS chronicling the making of the cult television show also published by Pioneer Books.
Mr. Altman's articles have also been featured in the BOSTON GLOBE and the JUSTICE. Altman served as editor-in-chief and co-publisher of GALACTIC JOURNAL MAGAZINE for nearly ten years.
Among his other credits are the screenplays for MOVING TARGETS and its sequel, MOVING TARGETS II. He recently finished work on a new supenatural thriller.
Altman, a transplanted New Yorker, now makes his home in Southern California (sorry, Woody) where he still has his Winnie The Pooh clock. Rumor has it he really wants to direct.

THE WOODY ALLEN ENCYCLOPEDIA

INTRODUCTION:

FROM STARUDST MEMORIES:

CHARLOTTE: What do you think the significance of the Rolls Royce was?

LAWYER: I think that it, uh, represents his car.

There's certainly no lack of books about Woody Allen. No, there are enough to fill up a small library (or even a big library). As prolific as Woody Allen - the filmmaker is, the cottage industry that has sprung up around him to analyze his work has been equally busy churning out untold pages examining his psyche and psychosis, new films and neurosis, libido and lobsters.

So why write another one? Next to Alfred Hitchcock, who has spawned a similar number of less than provocative tomes about his films, Allen's work has never ceased to fascinate critics who have pontificated at length about his "genius" in a myriad books ranging from the engaging "The Films of Woody Allen" by Robert Benyoun to the recent biography "Woody Allen" by Eric Lax in which Allen simply expounds the same old lines we've been hearing from the him for the last decade without offering considerably new insight into the real Woody Allen although it's still a great read.

The danger in writing a book about Allen to any film critic or fan (as I count myself) is to avoid the danger of sounding like the egomaniacal jerk who taught television at Columbia in ANNIE HALL who prattles on endlessly to his date about Fellini and Marshall McLuhan. As any Woody Allen fan knows, Allen rebuffs this man by having McLuhan literally rebuke him in the lobby of a crowded movie theater.

In other words, it's a dangerous game when you analyze a filmmakers intents and motives and, of course, the deeper meaning of their work — especially while they're still alive to

"just what the world needs, another book about woody allen"

disagree. But what differentiates Woody Allen's work from that of someone like Mel Brooks is that there is something deeper and more compelling that demands us to sit up and take notice rather than simply chortle and dismiss the film to the nether regions of our subconscious. Clearly, no one has or ever will give a great deal of thought to "Symbolism in SPACEBALLS" nor should they, but mention MANHATTAN and you're likely to evoke some very interesting pre-dinner conversation.

In my mind, some of the more penetrating critical work on Allen has missed the boat by zealously overscrutinizing films that are simply meant to make the audience laugh as much of his early work did and doesn't really offer anything on a deeper or more allegorical level. It was when Woody Allen was still a comic and not a philosopher or rather still being comic in his films rather than philosophizing. As a result, THE WOODY ALLEN COMPANION which you now hold in your hands takes the high road...and the low road. You'll find some fascinating commentary by film critic/filmmaker David Ian Salter in "8 1/2 STARDUSTED MEMORIES", one of the freshest approaches to the decade old controversy as to whether Allen produced a flattering homage to Fellini or a depressing rip-off assassinating his fans. On a lighter note, Mitch Rubinstein provides his own hommage to Woody Allen in his New Yorker-esque essay "AN AMERICAN DENTAL STUDENT IN LONDON" and some penetrating anaylsis by Thomas Doherty of Allen's personal favorite, THE PURPLE ROSE OF CAIRO and ALICE. Most of the text is taken up by the "ALLEN ENCYCLOPEDIA" researched in part by Allen fan Diane Eisenberg which provides a guide to the who's who and what's what of the Allen filmography. Why do you need an encyclopedia of Woody Allen's films. Well, actually I'm not sure, but it should prove helpful when dinner party conversations start to flounder and you find that your Allen knowledge isn't up to speed because you don't know who Martin Geist is.

Together we will revisit some of the funniest and most profound films made in the last two decades...and hopefully have a few laughs along the way.

A PRIMER

Alvie Singer (WOODY ALLEN) and Annie Hall (DIANE KEATON) talk as they walk after meeting for the first time on a tennis court in "ANNIE HALL"

CHAPTER ONE:

"a woody allen primer for the neophyte fan or the recently lobotomized"

By Mark A. Altman

THE EARLY, FUNNY YEARS

As the story goes, and has been told several times too many, Allen grew up in Brooklyn born Allen Stewart Konigsberg. Hardly the nerdy social outcast that he has been pegged as by many filmgoers, Allen was athletic and, not surprisingly, quite funny. He had a penchant for visiting the local cinema and soon found himself cutting classes to make midday excursions into Manhattan to visit its glittering movie palaces of the time. While still in school, Allen began contributing gags to Manhattan-based gag-writers and soon began to freelance as a gag-writer. While his school work suffered, his comedic work began to find its way into many popular columns . One column Allen contributed to was Earl Wilson's. This led to a stint writing for Sid Caesar where Allen worked with such funnymen as Mel Brooks and M*A*S*H's Larry Gelbart. In 1962, Allen began to perform on the stand-up circuit after meeting with limited success on the Borscht Belt Circuit in the Catskill Mountain's where the audience was particularly responsive to his unique brand of Jewish humor. Despite meeting initial setbacks, he became popular across the country making frequent appearances on the Johnny Carson show. He was regularly spotted plying his trade at the Duplex in Greenwich Village (or Greenberg's Village as Diane Keaton mistakenly calls it in SLEEPER), the Blue Angel, the Bitter End and the Hungry i in San Francisco. His managers, Jack Rollins and Charles H. Joffe, often forced a petrified Allen on-stage at many of his gigs but soon realized their faith was not misplaced. In a business where success often leads a celebrity to drop their manager and agent to move on to a bigger agency, Allen has shown loyalty. Even today he continues a long, fruitful and profitable association.

Some of Allen's most famous routines evolved during his stint as a stand-up comedian. While his stand-up comedy albums are notoriously difficult to obtain, his material is familiar to almost any Allen fan. Jokes about Allen flunking out of NYU for cheating on a metaphysics final when he was caught looking into the soul of the student next to him have subsequently made it into his film work. That particular anecdote was used in *ANNIE HALL* when Allen plays a stand-up comic. The familiar comedy staple of harraunging ones ex-wife got Allen into trouble when his repeated references to his first wife and teenage sweetheart, Harlene Rosen, resulted in a lawsuit. "My first wife, Quasimodo, was not officially animal. She was officially reptile. She's one of the few White Muslims in New York...Quasimodo and I were married by a reformed rabbi. Very reformed...He was a Nazi. She was very immature...once while I was taking a bath, she came in and sank my boats." One laugh that had everyone smiling but his ex-wife occurred when Allen jokingly stated on the Carson show, "I saw my ex-wife the other day. I almost didn't recognize her because I'd never before seen her with her wrists closed." And unlike Allen's favorite comedian of the time, the acerbic Mort Sahl, whose act consisted of politically biting social commentary, Allen's humor was grounded in daily life and personal interaction. Allen shied away from politics like the plague although once, in an out-

rageously hysterical 1968 television special, he engaged in a mock-debate with William F. Buckley. But probably Allen's most famous routine of all is the story of the Berkowitzes. In it, he relates a great moose hunt. "I shot a moose," goes the story. "It was alive. There is a law in New York State against driving with a live moose on your fender, on Tuesday, Thursday or Saturday." Taking the moose to a costume party and introducing it as the Solomons, the moose won second place for Best Costume being bested by the Berkowitzes who came dressed as a moose. Woody then took the moose back to the woods, but it was actually the Berkowitzes "and there's a law in New York against driving with Jews on your fender on Tuesday, Thursday and especially Saturday." The moose gets shot and Mr. Berkowitz is stuffed and hung on the wall of the New York Athletic Club, but "the jokes on them, because the place is restricted." Not surprisingly, some of Allen's most effective humor in his early films is derived from his narration and the verbal humor he felt most comfortable with. It wasn't u*SLEEPER* that he was able to successfully meld his aptitude for verbal humor with a flair for physical comedy. Abetted by an excellent use of jazz riffs for accompaniment, *SLEEPER* possesses some of the wittiest slapstick humor ever to appear in a Woody Allen movie. Allen's entry into Hollywood was the result of his being recruited by producer Charles K. Feldman who hired him to write the screenplay for *WHAT'S NEW, PUSSYCAT?* (1965), a dismally inane film which was extremely popular at the time of its release. While Allen, who appears in the film, is one of the most amusing elements,.the talents of Peter O'Toole and Peter Sellers cannot save it. O'Toole plays a high fashion magazine editor who's about to get married but cannot give up his playboy ways. In CASINO ROYALE (1967), Feldman's idiotic take-off on the James Bond series, Allen returns as a gun (or is that `gub'?) for hire Allen plays Jimmy Bond, a.k.a. Dr. Noah. Bent on world conquest, he renders all the worlds' women beautiful and kills all men over 4'6". Allen, having failed to assassinate Sir James Bond (David Niven) kidnaps his daughter, Mata Bond (Joanna Pettet) and takes her to his secret base under Monte Carlo. He captures one of Bond's agents, the beautiful Daliah Lavi, whom he strips and binds to a table. Informing her about his secret plans, he reveals an atomic bomb in tablet form which contains 400 tiny time pills. Feigning an interest in him, Lavi drops the tablet in his champagne which Allen drinks and four hundred hiccups later, he explodes taking the entire cast with him. Allen, not surprisingly, is once again the best thing about the film which is a hodge-podge of scenes concocted by several directors (John Huston, Kenneth Hughes, Val Guest, Robert Parrish, Joseph McGrath). These directors seemed to be working without any idea of what the other was doing.

Like the DeLaurentiis' films of today, Feldman was an old-time producer who felt that if you throw enough money up on the screen, the script doesn't matter. Despite the contribution of DR. NO writer, Wolf Mankowitz, the script was a mess. But there's a sucker born every minute, not every second, and even CASINO ROYALE couldn't fool the filmgoers of America into thinking this film was any good. Filled with scantily clad women (including Bond babe Ursula Andress and Pussycat's Romy Schneider) and double entendres that were a staple of the Bond spoof genre (which ranged from Dean Martin's MATT HELM films to James Coburn's FLINT films), CASINO ROYALE was the worst of the bunch. Ironically, it would be the next Woody Allen film that would be the best Bond spoof yet. "WHAT'S UP TIGER LILY?" (1966), was a Japanese martial arts film, KAGI NO KAGI, which Allen redubbed with his cronies including comedian and voiceover artist extraordinarre Len Maxwell, former wife Louise Lasser and Mickey Rose, a high school buddy with whom Allen collaborated with frequently in the early days of his film career. While attending Congressional hearings against colorization in 1989, a rare public appearance for Allen, he was asked whether what he did to "WHAT'S UP TIGER LILY?" was analogous to what Ted Turner was doing by tampering with classic black & white films. Allen said, "I was young back then. I wouldn't do it again." Although only 79 minutes, TIGER LILY'S greatest fault is it's length. Trimmed to 55 minutes or so it would be a hoot, but at 79 the movie's amusing antics quickly grow tiresome despite the bevy of outrageous dialogue that Woody and Company contrived for the production. "Two Wongs don't make a right," one spy tells the evil villain Wing Fat as Phil Moskowitz, lovable rogue, our hero searches for the secret recipe for egg salad. While in Europe shooting CASINO ROYALE, Allen was productive as he sat around waiting to be called to the set as the massive film went over-schedule and over-budget. In addition to writing some witty contributions to the New Yorker (since collected in the three books, GETTING EVEN, SIDE EFFECTS and WITHOUT FEATHERS), Allen wrote his first Broadway play, DON'T DRINK THE WATER, in which an American family visiting a mythical Iron Curtain country called Vulgaria are mistakenly suspected of being spies. The play, which opened to mixed notices was adapted into a 1969 film starring Jackie Gleason and Estelle Parsons. Instead of shooting abroad, Vulgaria was recreated in Miami Beach because like Allen, who now has the clout to refuse to shoot out of New York, Gleason insisted on filming on his home turf of Miami. But it would be TAKE THE MONEY AND RUN (1969) in which Allen would first have the opportunity to achieve the rank of cinematic auteur. Allen not only starred as criminal Virgil Starkwell, but co-wrote and directed TAKE THE MONEY AND RUN which according to Allen was destined to destroy his film career until editor Ralph Rosenblum intervened to give the film structure and save it Ultimately, it would be Vincent Canby's glowing review in the NEW YORK TIMES which would save the film from obscurity and elevate Allen into the pantheon of pop culture heroes on the rise.

"TAKE THE MONEY AND RUN" is filled with some of Allen's funniest one-liners and was shot on a modest budget of $2 million. A scene in which Virgil attempts to rob a bank but is met with resistance when the teller can't read his penmanship on a holdup note and mistakes Allen's gun for a gub, is unforgettable. Allen brought the film in under budget and under schedule. The film is a very primitive version of a technique Allen would later master in ZELIG, the mock-documentary. Shot in San Francisco for budgetary reasons, Allen shot at San Quentin where cast and crew intermingled with actual inmates. A far cry from the protected Kaufman-Astoria studio sets filled with gleaming sitting rooms and up-scale Manhattan locales of his 80's films. Janet Margolin stars as Virgil's love, Louise, and it would be one of the only times (Charlotte Rampling in STARDUST MEMORIES was another) that a lead in a Woody Allen comedy was not played by a leading lady in his personal life. Margolin essentially plays a straight woman to Allen's antics as he tries to pass himself off as a cellist in the New York Philharmonic.

Woody also gives his self-reflexive tendencies free reign. Having often cannibalized the cinema as a source of inspiration and sometimes redemption (as was the case in HANNAH AND HER SISTERS), director Allen alludes to such prison-break classics as THE DEFIANT ONES, I AM A FUGITIVE FROM A CHAIN GANG and COOL HAND LUKE. Importantly, one of the most outstanding and blatant cinematic allusions in the film was eventually excised. In homage to BONNIE & CLYDE, Virgil is shot down bloodily in a slow-motion coda to the comedic gangster saga and the ending was dropped as being inappropriate. Instead the film ends neatly when Allen, attempting to rob an old friend on a side-street overlooking the West Side Highway, finds out his high school buddy is a police officer and is arrested. It's an impressive debut and although Allen's visual technique was less than par and the editing extremely choppy, it works.

In 1971, Woody Allen began his relationship with United Artists and the executive team whom would grant him unprecedented creative freedom (years later he would follow them to Orian). His first film under his UA agreement was the outrageous political satire BANANAS, originally entitled "El Weirdo". The film is the story of what one man will do to impress a beautiful girl. Fielding Mellish (Allen) after meeting, falling in love and being dumped by a political activist (Louise Lasser) flies off to the Banana Republic of San Marcos to impress her. Once there, Mellish becomes embroiled in a plot by rebels to overthrow the Marxist government. But when the rebel leader lets power go to his head and is even more dictatorial than Vargas, his predecessor Fielding, is asked to take over the country as leader. From the opening moment's, BANANAS is one of Allen's most outrageous motion pictures. Howard Cosell offers color commentary of a political assassination from which the film segues into a spirited title sequence and a hysterically conceived series of mishaps. We are introduced to Mellish, a product tester for a major corporation who stops at the local newsstand to pick up a copy of "Orgasm". On the train, he attempts to help an elderly lady who is being mugged by thugs (one of which is RAMBO, Sylvester Stallone) which turns out badly for the poor schlemiel.

In 1972, Allen starred in the adaptation of his 1969 Broadway play PLAY IT AGAIN SAM, in which Herbert Ross directed him and what would later turn into a stable of regular players, Diane Keaton and Tony Roberts in another winning comedy. Allen hoped Richard Benjamin would play the perennial putz, Allan Felix, but when he was not available, Allen was forced to assume the role himself.

PLAY IT AGAIN SAM defined the Woody Allen persona which continues to plague the talented auteur who has celebrated his 50th birthday. That of the nerdy and insecure neurotic who can't seem to "score" with women. Allen has aged gracefully and lost the freckled face innocence of his youth. He is clearly a cul-tured and sophisticated man of great taste possessing a bevy of talents ranging from director to writer to musician.

In order to overcome his problems in the film, Allen's Allan Felix enlists the aid of the consummate male image, Humphrey Bogart (Jerry Lacy), to tutor him in virile sophistication. Although Felix's best-friend, Dick Christie (played with comic gusto by Tony Roberts) attempts to introduce him to a variety of eligible vixens, he ends up falling for his friend's wife, Linda (Diane Keaton). She is the only woman he feels comfortable with and is not threatened by. Inspired by his favorite film, CASABLANCA, Felix eventually bids adieu urging Linda to join her husband on a departing plane. The film fanatic finally gets to live out his dream, even if it means losing the girl because its the right thing to do. Ross's film lacks the staginess and confinement of many less successful play adaptations. Allen wisely discards THE MALTESE FALCON and THE BIG SLEEP, the framing devices used in the play, instead taking CASABLANCA as the model which Felix follows. SAM also features the memorable series of phonecalls by Tony Roberts to his service letting them know where he can be reached next.

The film is a perennial favorite for Allen fans and more conventional and accessible than his other films for non-Woodyholics. It follows a traditional Hollywood structure and fails to probe the barriers of technique that Allen's earlier auteured ventures had. Yet, it embraces a fundamental issue which will characterize many of Allen's 70's works, how do I know if women want to have sex? What do women want from a man and how do I get laid? It's a pivotal question Allen has yet to provide an answer to. In SAM, Felix is paired with a nymphomaniac who tantalizes him by saying, "sex is something that should happen as often and freely as possible". When he attempts to follow-up on that proposition, she screams and runs out of the apartment yelling "What do you take me for?".

Woody's female troubles seem to emanate from sex being an elusive commodity leading him to ponder his failings for nearly a decade — long after abstinence has replaced promiscuity as the reigning philosophy.

Today, Woody is constantly reinventing himself. Labelled a misogynist by the feminist left who decried his anti-feminist tirades in his early work, Allen has stated more recently that "women are a better class of people then men" .He has abandoned the complaints of the young, uninteresting nerd and taken the high-road by probing the psyche of the troubled working woman of the contemporary middle and upper classes in his 80's work.

Few of Allen's works tackled sex in a more direct manner than his adaptation of Dr. David Reuben's best selling self-help sex manual, EVERYTHING YOU ALWAYS WANTED TO KNOW ABOUT SEX* (*BUT WERE AFRAID TO ASK). This 1972 film was comprised of a series of vignettes drawn from chapters of Reuben's book. But rather than tackle the non-fiction theories, Allen extrapolated outrageously off-color storylines. Although Allen's manager, Charles Joffe promised that the film wouldn't be a "nudie or a lewdie", the final film disappointed the book's author. In an interview with the L.A. Herald-Examiner he said he disliked the film because it was a "sexual tragedy". "Every episode in the picture was a chronicle of sexual failure," he stated, "which was the converse of

everything in the book." It was Allen's first film to receive an R rating despite being devoid of any profanity or nudity (RADIO DAYS, ironically, has the distinction of being the only Woody Allen film to feature any nudity). And although the film was generally lambasted on its release for its ribald and generally tastelessly funny humor, some critics appreciated the fact that it was the first film in which Allen embraced a discernible filmic style. Actually, a series of styles. Allen's mis en scene reflected the styles of the genres he parodied in each segment and the visuals mimicked the look of some very distinctive films. In the opening segment "Do Aphrodisiacs Work?", a medieval court jester (Allen) is told by his father's ghost to seduce the queen (Lynn Redgrave) and goes to the resident sorcerer (Geoffrey Holder) for a love potion, but when he puts his moves on the queen his hand gets trapped in her chastity belt just as the king (Anthony Quayle) arrives in her bedchamber. Tragically, Allen is beheaded.

Woody Allen's definition of "What is Sodomy?" is not one you'll hear very often and although easily recalled by most people talking about the film, the segment is pretty awful. In it, a Jewish doctor (Gene Wilder) confronts a Greek immigrant, Mr. Milos (Titos Vandis) who has fallen in love with his sheep, Daisy. At first Wilder is appalled, but soon falls in love with the sheep himself and even goes to bed with it. He is ultimately divorced by his wife and left penniless on the street drinking a bottle of Woolite.

More memorable is the sequence on "Why Do Some Women Have Trouble Reaching Orgasm?" In it, Woody spoofs the films of Antonioni and Fellini's "La Dolce Vita", both literally in the segment's visual motifs and its story which is in Italian with English subtitles. He plays the suave Italian stud ala Marcello Mastrioanni who is married to a beautiful, voluptuous wife (played by, of all people, Louise Lasser). But despite several attempts to arouse her in bed, Woody is unsuccessful until they embrace in a boutique and have passionate sex. Allen soon realizes his wife can only come to orgasm in public places where's there's danger of being caught. Although the segment never really resolves in any discernible dramatic fashion, the simple premise is amusingly abetted by the Italian Neo-Realist technique employed by Allen in shooting the segment.

Less engaging is "Are Transvestites Homosexuals" in which familiar character actor Lou Jacobi plays Sam, who along with his wife, visit the parents of his daughter's fiancee. During a dull dinner conversation, Sam sneaks up to the parents room and absconds with the woman's clothing dressing in drag. When he is almost discovered, he flees out the window onto the street and is mugged. An ensuing flurry of attention is diverted to Sam who is trying fruitlessly to get back into the house and discard his female accoutrements. Ultimately, there's no payoff to the piece and aside from the visual gag of seeing Michael "time to make the donuts" Vale look-alike, Jacobi in drag dancing in front of a mirror, the segment is thoroughly unfunny.

In "What Are Sex Perverts", Allen contributes one of his most amusing segments in which game show host Jack Barry plays the m.c. of a kinescoped gameshow, "What's My Perversion". Regis Philbin and a panel of experts attempt to guess a man's perversion (for the record, he enjoys exposing himself on the subway), but the real kicker is the write-in winner, a rabbi who asks to be tied up and beaten by a shapely shiksa while his wife lies at his feet eating pork.

Allen tackles the films of Roger Corman, 50's B science-fiction movies and the classic Universal horror films in "Are The Findings Of Doctors And Clinics Who Do Sexual Research Accurate". Allen plays Victor Shakapopolis (his character in WHAT'S NEW PUSSYCAT) who on his way to see Dr. Bernardo (John Carradine) is joined by a pretty female reporter (Heather MacRae) who is on her way to do a story on Bernardo's sex research clinic. They quickly discover that the doctor is quite mad when he plans, as his crowning achievement, to monitor the reporter's response to being gangbanged by a pack of Cub Scouts while he injects silicon into a flat chested woman to create larger breasts. Allen seems to exorcise his adolescent wish-fulfillment in this segment which is filled with sexual banter and experimentation bordering on the perverse (a man has sex with a large rye bread). When Allen destroys the lab, he finds to his horror that a giant breast has been released which is ravaging the countryside. Allen saves the day by devising a brilliant plan to capture the breast by building a better brassiere. The story ends with our two heroes in a passionate embrace on a mountain as the sun sets on the horizon echoing the unforgettable imagery of GONE WITH THE WIND.

However, unquestionably the best sequence in the film is "What Happens During Ejaculation?". Tony Randall, Woody Allen and Burt Reynolds star in this take-off on FANTASTIC VOYAGE in which Allen plays a sperm who isn't sure if he's going to be called into action during a hot date. Meanwhile, in the command center,

Randall coordinates a variety of body functions in the young male on the date while putting the moves on an eligible young woman. It's by far the funniest story in the film in which both the visual and verbal humor only serve to the benefit of the story.

Excised from the final cut was "What Makes A Man A Homosexual?" in which Woody plays a spider who is made love to and then eaten by another spider personified by Louise Lasser. The process is observed by a gay scientist also played by Woody who comes to the conclusion that women are truly deadly.

In 1973, Woody Allen woke up from 200 years in suspended animation in SLEEPER in which he finds himself in an America very different than the one he left. The society is a police state where everything is mechanized and controlled. But rather than comment on the totalitarian state and the prevalent human attitudes of 1973 which allowed this world to exist, Allen milks the situation for all the comic material he can — which is quite alot. Escaping from the secret police, Allen disguises himself as a service robot where he works for Luna (Diane Keaton), a pathetic poetess. When he reveals he is actually the "alien" the police are looking for, she tries to turn him in, but when they try to kill her too, Luna comes to accept the wisdom of the underground attempting to overthrow the government. Meanwhile, Allen's Miles Monroe, having been captured, and transformed into the perfect citizen is kidnapped by the underground. Luna and her lover Erno (John Beck), the rebel leader, attempt to revive Mile's reprogrammed memories by playing out the roles of his parents as they exchange stilted Yiddish dialogue preceding the Passover Seder. Ultimately, Miles and Luna

penetrate the leader's headquarters and discover that the leader has been killed by a rebel bomb, but doctors are attempting to clone his nose to save their regime. SLEEPER is Allen's most accomplished film to that time and he ably employs the familiar self-reflexive trappings of the genre we've grown accustomed to with familiar references to such books as Edward Bellamy's LOOKING BACKWARDS and Orwells 1984. He also exhibits a newfound ability for physical comedy (First, he attempts to steal giant vegetables. Later he is pursued in an inflatable spacesuit by police as he bounces off into the distance and in the guise of the robot embarks on routines worthy of the masters of silent screen comedy). Some of the contraptions Woody envisions in his personal future shock are bawdy and riotous. an example is the orgasamitron, a substitute for sex whereby two people step into a machine and experience immediate sexual satisfaction.

Directorally, Allen seems more comfortable with the camera. the images he creates are more arresting than any of his previous screen comedies and the story shows a narrative thread lacking from his previous efforts. The props and sets all service his comic take on this futureworld and rather than resort to high tech realism such as is found in 2001, and partially because of budget constraints, he showcases pulpy sets which suit the material well.

Although SLEEPER is set 200 years in the future, it is more akin to BANANAS than any of the sci-fi it pays homage to. The only successful cloning operation is SLEEPER's transplant of the Fielding Mellish character from BANANAS into Miles Monroe. When Luna tells Monroe that he believes in nothing, Allen replies "Sex and death. Two things that occur once in life." Monroe's sentiments, which recalled Mellish's personal philosophy in BANANAS, are virtually identical. Their personalities and many of SLEEPER'S scenes appear to be new and improved versions of scenes from his previous venture. Illustrating the constant evolution of Allen's abilities. In BANANAS, Fielding's activities in the rebel camp echo those of Monroe's transformation into the rebel hero in SLEEPER and even Keaton's off-key rebel anthem "Rebels Are We" makes a return appearance from Allen's former laughfest.

LOVE & DEATH (1975) represents a transitional point for Allen, who having mastered the broad physical comedy featuring outrageous situations (perfecting his unique brand of BANANAS humor in SLEEPER), returned to a literary inspired mode utilizing a more intellectually challenging verbal humor in creating "LOVE AND DEATH" Allen plays Boris, a cowardly soldier who accidently becomes a hero in the war against Napoleon and is finally able to marry his cousin Sonia (Diane Keaton) who recruits him in a plan to assassinate Napoleon. LOVE & DEATH is a finely woven, costumed period piece which Allen shot in Budapest, Hungary, far from the shores of native New York. Among the many allusions Allen draws are to Tolstoy's WAR & PEACE and Bergman's SEVENTH SEAL in which Death incarnate brings Woody face to face with the grim reality of death.

LOVE & DEATH balances the filmmaker's two greatest obsessions; sex and death in an amusing take on Russian literature. While not his most amusing broad comedy, and his more sophomoric humor sometimes misses the target, the film marks the end of the first Woody Allen era which began with TAKE THE MON-

EY AND RUN and paved the way for the films that would follow.

GENIUS UNLEASHED

Allen's second film as an actor-for-hire was Martin Ritt's condemnation of the Hollywood blacklist and HUAC, "THE FRONT", an underrated entry in the Allen ouvere and an accomplished and powerful, if not preachy, film which is more important than it's given credit for. But it wasn't until 1977, the year that gave us STAR WARS, that one of Allen's greatest achievements was released to critical acclaim and Academy Award recognition. ANNIE HALL, originally entitled ANHEDONIA (inability to enjoy oneself), is a triumphant accomplishment for Allen. It successfully combines the dramatic and comedic strains in his work and is richly rewarding with compelling characters and deliciously delightful humor.

One person who has surprisingly not gotten the credit he deserves is co-writer Marshall Brickman. He worked with Allen on his two greatest films, yet is hardly given a footnote in most of the works. Together, Brickman and Allen fashioned a murder mystery set in New York, but CLUE was not what resulted. Over four hours of footage were pared down to 93 minutes and the classic romantic 70's comedy was born.

But beyond simply looking at relationships in the post-Aquarius age, Allen also introduced us to his New York. A city which would return in many of his future films and become the most visible and significant character in his body of work.

A familiar theme probed most successfully in ANNIE HALL dealt with the age-old New York versus Los Angeles rivalry and Allen's distaste for the Left Coast bordered on physical repugnance. While Annie is swept up by the shallowness of 70's California culture and record producer Tony Lacey (Paul Simon) based on Warren Beatty, Allen assumes the mantle of chief spokesman for the city of New York. He has chanted the Manhattan mantra for years, but ANNIE HALL is his most scathing look at its sister city of the west. In one scene, Alvy Singer's first trip to L.A. is during Christmas. The sun shines brightly on the Palm Trees even as the Christmas decorations and music fill the late December morning. He introduces the classic dichotomy which was plumbed in such films as LETHAL WEAPON and DIE HARD which undercut the classic iconography of snow covered hills with the hot sun of a winter's day in L.A.. Allen establishes the stereotype of the cultured New Yorker and the shallow California narcissist and nowhere does he do it better than in ANNIE HALL.with Tony Roberts' Rob playing a transplanted New York actor who has been consumed by the California lifestyle. Rob has given up the hopes and aspirations he once had as a struggling New York actor and has given into the financially and sexually fulfilling, if shallow, California way of life. No filmmaker has more successfully reinforced the stereotype of West Coast living than Woody Allen.

ANNIE HALL, Allen's first screen comedy set in the real world rather than Allen's reel world in which comedy dictates substance as opposed to the reverse, still leans on a number of filmic crutches to service his goals. Such devices as Allen turning to the audience and looking out from the proscenium conversing with the audience or intermittently reminding us that we're watching a film harkens back to his earlier work.

Allen's Alvy Singer has several sexual conquests (he's married twice in the film) in ANNIE HALL and ultimately transcends his failings through his art. In the final scenes, despite failing to reach a reproachment with his ex-lover, Annie, jury rigs their floundering relationship in a play he writes where Annie comes back to him begging to be a part of his life again. This reaffirms the Allen philosophy prevalent in all his early work in which women are incomprehensible and unpredictable and only controllable through fiction.

Only through his play can Alvy make his relationship with Annie turn out the way he wants it to because despite all his best attempts to reconcile, she rebuffs him, and only through the fiction of film can Allen create a world in which women are receptive to his comic persona. Only in Woody's world, are Jewish wit and wisdom enough to attract a beautiful, intellectually stimulating single woman. In the real world, it's considerably more complicated he tells us by implication.

In 1978 Allen embarked on his most ambitious undertaking,INTERIORS, which has attracted its fair share of critical barbs over the years. INTERIORS set the tone for the serious work that would come later. After the financial success of ANNIE HALL, the studio was willing to allow Allen to do a long desired serious drama which would not feature him in it. One of the complaints that has been directed at INTERIORS is that Woody's pendulum swung too far in the opposite direction, not only is it not a comedy, but there's nothing remotely funny or humorous about it. It's no wonder everyone wants to commit suicide in this movie.

Ultimately, the film's theme addresses a woman, Joey (Mary Beth Hurt) who possesses many worldly concerns but lacks the talent to be able to express them through art. Eve (Geraldine Page), the mother of three daughters is told suddenly by her husband Arthur (E.G. Marshall) that he wishes to spend some time on his own and asks for a trial separation. Although, Arthur has no intention of coming back to his former wife, the daughters - with the exception of Joey - lead their mother to believe that one day he will return to her.

The ensemble is filled with a number of talented performers including Richard Jordan as Frederick, the husband of Renata (Diane Keaton) who is a frustrated author who watched his wife succeed as a poetess and resents her success, Sam Waterston as Mike, Joey's husband and newcomer Kristen Griffith, who plays Flynn, the youngest daughter who is a successful television actress. Woody seems to flounder in an element he's unfamiliar with, the WASP middle class.

As opposed to his familiar Jewish canvas, Allen attempts to delve into high-minded upper middle class WASP life and although he makes a noble attempt, the dialogue is at times stilted and forced and the finale in which the father seeks one daughter's approval who seeks her mother's approval while the successful daughter seeks her father's approval is hardly subtle stuff. Perhaps the problem is that while his earlier work is so effective in penetrating the concerns of the enlightened Everyman, few can actually relate to the dilemmas which plague these characters and Allen does not make their world engaging enough for us to care.

Unquestionably, the influence of the Bergman filmography on the film is ever-present and perhaps one day Allen will be able to address Bergman-esque themes without using his cinematic techniques. In INTERIORS, he's like the kid who gets a Super 8 Camera for his birthday and rushes out to shoot his first horror movie by asking his girlfriend to step into the shower while pouring red food coloring down the drain. Analogously, Allen takes his Panavision and gets to dupe his favorite filmmaker. Despite its problems, INTERIORS is a visual feast and Gordon Willis' cinematography is stunning. Ultimately, we are surprised by the fact that the frequent object of Allen's barbs, puzzled self-indulgent intellectuals, have now become one of affection and concern.

Allen's crowning achievement, and greatest film to date is his love anthem to New York, MANHATTAN (1979). This lovingly rendered story of a successful television writer, Isaac Davis (Allen) who quits his job to write the "Great American Novel" and, more importantly create a work of art. Ironically, Allen who had given up on comedy which he likened to "sitting at the kiddie table" to create a "great work of art" with serious drama in INTERIORS proved ill-conceived whereas with MANHATTAN he achieves his goal.

In MANHATTAN, Allen created his masterpiece. It's a term that should be used sparingly and one that should be used even less in describing the popular cinema, but like CITIZEN KANE, NOTORIOUS, CASABLANCA, THE SWEET SMELL OF SUCCESS, THE SEVENTH SEAL and THE GODFATHER, MANHATTAN is truly one of the greatest films ever made. Allen had finally created a great work of art, although he denies that he has to this day.

Shot in black and white, Gordon Willis' magnificent cinematography presents a city which could only exist in art ranging from the 59th Street Bridge at dawn to the Hayden Planetarium to Central Park. The familiar police sirens, litter and crime which are the price all New Yorkers must pay for living in the world's greatest city are not to be found in Allen's film. In fact, a sound effect in which a mugging is overheard by Isaac and Tracy (Mariel Hemingway) as they take a romantic carriage ride in the park was omitted by Allen who felt it would ruin the illusion of the city as he was trying to portray it.

MANHATTAN is a microcosm of New York in the 70's and the prevailing attitudes of the time. Unlike ANNIE HALL which although funny is at times crude in its cinematic technique, MANHATTAN is beautifully realized in its wide screen format and the Gershwin score supports the pulsating images on the screen. Also, while ANNIE HALL pitted New York against Los Angeles, MANHATTAN took Allen's idealized version of Manhattan and presented it alongside the real New York outside the theater doors.

MANHATTAN is filled with a bevy of superb supporting performances including Michael Murphy as Isaac's friend Yale, Meryl Streep as his ex-wife turned lesbian writer and Mariel Hemingway who is innocent and vulnerable as Tracy, Isaac's 17 year old girlfriend.

Similar to ANNIE HALL, and most of Allen's work, the ending is ambiguous and certainly not the happy ending we've come to expect in the cinema. Yet, Woody avoids having his affair with a young girl become a Lolita-like affair. Woody's motives seem purer than Hubert Humberts and we never get the sense of Isaac as lecherous or sleazy.

Having been rejected by Mary (Diane Keaton) who has returned to enjoying an adulterous affair with Isaac's friend Yale, Allen attempts to reconcile with Tracy who is on her way to England. Is the spark of true love rekindling or is a pathetic man desperately trying to hold onto his lost youth and avoid loneliness? There isn't an easy answer, but outside the city rythms continue and thousands of other stories in the Naked City go on.

Fortunately, a few of them are still going to be Woody's. STARDUST MEMORIES (1980) is one of Allen's most controversial films. Perceived as a jab at his fans who clamored for him to return to his early, funny films, STARDUST MEMORIES is filled with ambiguities and although overflowing with flashbacks and films within films, it is probably one of his most successful offbeat entries. Whether Sandy Bates really is a thinly veiled Woody Allen (and he says he isn't) isn't important. It's a witty and intriguing film.

Inspired by Fellini's 8 1/2, Allen's American retelling of a filmmakers odyssey doesn't elicit much sympathy for Sandy, but it does provoke some amusement. If Bates is truly to be trusted as providing us with a subjective view of what Woody sees and fears, then STARDUST MEMORIES lends us fascinating insight into the mind of the troubled auteur. Unfortunately, when the aliens come down and tell Allen/Bates that he should stop worrying about the nature of the Universe and just make funnier films, that's what he's good at, we think Allen finally gets the picture and forgive him for disparaging his fans in such a ruthless and grotesque manner. He doesn't though. The aliens are just as foolish as the studio in trying to convince the filmmaker to accept the wisdom of their words and stick to what he's good at. It may appear that Allen has heeded their advice, but in a midsummer night in SEPTEMBER he'll have the last laugh. You know, jazz heaven didn't sound so bad.

THE ORION YEARS

Intending to undertake an ambitious new film, a mock-documentary, Allen started doing his homework after the completion of STARDUST MEMORIES. Realizing he had time to do one film before that film would be ready to go before the cameras, Allen hastily wrote and scheduled his version of Bergman's SMILES OF A SUMMER'S NIGHT, his first film for Orion Pictures.

Allen's loyal supporters in the UA hierarchy had jumped ship to start Orion Pictures and Allen joined them at the fledgling independent which distributed its pictures through Warner Bros. MIDSUMMER also introduced us to Allen's new love who would become a regular staple of his ouvere, Mia Farrow. She stars in MIDSUMMER with Julie Hagerty, Tony Roberts, Jose Ferrer and Mary Steenburgen and hardly shows the signs of what a valued member of the Allen company she would later display in her more accomplished performances.

A MIDSUMMER NIGHTS SEX COMEDY (1982) is one of the low-points of Allen's comedic career. It's a turn of the century farce in which Allen plays a bumbling inventor. Totally out of place, Allen's contemporary veneer and mannerisms rendered him incompatible with the surroundings he had devised and most importantly, MIDSUMMER is simply not funny. Again we see an ensemble looking

for love in all the wrong places. Set out in a magic woods, MIDSUMMER seems like INTERIORS taken outdoors and injected with some stale humor, a turn of the century EXTERIORS.

But the unpleasant intermission was easily forgotten in the wake of his next effort, the utterly brilliant mock-documentary ZELIG (1983) which tells the imaginary story through a series of fake newsreels and footage of Leonard Zelig, a man who underwent physical change to fit in with those around him. Zelig would suddenly transform into the person he was with whether it be an Indian, a black jazz musician or a Republican.

What is remarkable about the film is the way that actual newsreel footage is seamlessly blended into the fictitious tapestry Allen weaves. At a sparse 79 minutes, ZELIG is just right length and Patrick Horgan's narration utterly effective. ZELIG perfectly illustrated how much Allen had learned and grown as a filmmaker since making TAKE THE MONEY AND RUN. Although the film does make the occasional misstep seguing into traditional Allen humor such as, "I broke with Freud on the concept of penis envy, he felt it should be restricted to women" and "I have to get back to the University for my class on masturbation, I don't want them to start without me."

Perhaps the most delightful and telling moments in ZELIG are Allen's recreations of a fictional Warner Bros. film about Zelig, "The Changing Man". In it, Allen recaptures the style, look and performances of the films of the period and gloriously services the satire of the media age he has crafted with such precision.

In the atypical BROADWAY DANNY ROSE, Allen plays a small-time theatrical manager named Danny Rose who manages a number of bizarre acts including a blind xylophone player and a man whose birds play the piano. The genesis of the film reportedly springs from Mia Farrow who during a dinner one night told Allen that she wanted to play a character like the loud, chain-smoking blonde with sunglasses sitting next to them at a restaurant they were dining at. The film is framed by a number of classic comedians telling the "best" Danny Rose story; Corbett Monica, Morty Gunty (father of well-known casting director Lori Gunty), Jackie Gayle, Will Jordan, Howie Storm, Sandy Baron and Allen manager Jack Rollins. Nick Apollo Forte plays Lou Canova, a has-been singer whose career Danny Rose hopes to revive riding the cusp of a nostalgia craze. As a favor to Lou, Allen agrees to "beard" for him by taking his girlfriend to a big performance at the Waldorf Astoria which his wife will be attending. Rose through a series of comedic happenstance ends up being chased by the mob and, ultimately as so frequently happens in the talent business, abandoned by his star client when he achieves some degree of attention jumping to another agent.

While ROSE is hardly one of Allen's most impressive achievements, it's an amusing romp with a delightful performance from Farrow as Tina Vitale.

Allen's favorite movie THE PURPLE ROSE OF CAIRO was plagued by trouble at the start. Michael Keaton was to star as its dual protagonists. He would have played actor Gil Shepherd and character Tom Baxter who comes down one day from the movie screen when he falls in love with Cecilia (Mia Farrow), a depression-era movie junkie whose life is miserable except for her daily fix at the bi-

jou. Allen simply felt Keaton was too contemporary for the 1920's tale and replaced him with Jeff Daniels resulting in some substantial reshooting, par for the course for Allen at Orion.

CAIRO owes a debt to Allen's classic New Yorker piece "The Kugelmass Episode" which is read side by side in high schools today with "Madame Bovary" in which a humanities professor obsessed with the book transplants himself into the novel to become romantically involved with Bovary. Similarly, in PURPLE ROSE a fictitious character leaves his fantasy world and enters the real world obsessed with a woman he's seen in the theater.

Perhaps the reason that CAIRO was a box-office disappointment, if not an aesthetic one, was because of its downbeat ending. Rather than finding love with the Hollywood hero, Gil Shepherd, he abandons her once all is set right and Cecilia once again returns to seeking solace and abandoning the real world at the movies. Had Allen ended his film on a happier note, no doubt the box office would have been better, but Allen's art demands a resolve in which all does not end happily ever after. Certainly the movies are not a panacea for life's ills, only an aspirin — temporary relief from the pressing concerns of daily life, a theme he would return to in future work.

In 1986, Allen directed his most engaging effort since MANHATTAN, HANNAH & HER SISTERS. A critical and financial success, HANNAH is the story of Hannah (Mia Farrow) and her two sisters, one a struggling actor, Holly (Dianne Weist) and the other a misunderstood beauty with whom her husband, Elliot (Michael Caine) is in love with. Unlike the dull sisterly threesome of

INTERIORS, HANNAH tackles the same territory with a fresh and witty eye making HANNAH one of the most interesting of Allen's later works.

Once again splendidly cast by veteran casting director Juliet Taylor, HANNAH is a visual and verbal treat for the mind with Allen's sophisticated urban humor contemplating the many dilemmas life has to offer. As Mickey (Woody Allen), Woody comes face to face with his own mortality when after years as a long-suffering hypochondriac he is led to believe he has a brain tumor. Mickey ultimately finds out he's perfectly fine and after seeking salvation in religion finally finds it in laughter and the movies. It's a realization we can only hope Allen will make for himself sometime in the future.

Returning to his old comedic turf, Allen's RADIO DAYS (1987) is a giddy series of anecdotes recalling his youth spent listening to the radio and although it doesn't always hit its mark, it's a fun, little film. At a budget of $15 million, this period piece is his most expensive film and features a stable of Allen regulars ranging from Mia Farrow, Julie Kavner, Dianne Wiest, Jeff Daniels, Tony Roberts, Diane Keaton and most amusingly Wallace Shawn as the daredevil radio crusader the Masked Avenger.

Although not as funny as his earliest work, RADIO DAYS does feature some of his greatest bits including the opening scene in which two bumbling robbers answer the phone during a burglary where they are being called by "NAME THAT TUNE" mistaken for the residents of the house only to win the grand jackpot.

Allen's various antics as a youth looking to save up for a Masked Avenger decoder ring are equally riotous when he commandeers a collection box meant to support the establishment of Israel so that he can order a ring and is suitably castigated by the rabbi and his parents. The melancholy tone of the films coda in which Allen admits that his recollections of those pleasant memories of his formative years dim with every passing annum is a depressing reminder of how the passage of time erases not only bad, but good thoughts and a testament to Allen the filmmaker who has the ability to immortalize his youth for all future generations to share. And then came SEPTEMBER (1987), Allen's most boorish and absolutely annoying serious venture. Reshot twice with changes in casting that included Maureen O'Sullivan being replaced by Elaine Stritch, Charles Durning by Jack Warden and Sam Shepherd by Sam Waterston, SEPTEMBER is one of Allen's most profoundly awful efforts. It commits the highest crime and misdemeanor of being boring. In his biography on Woody Allen, Eric Lax describes the difficulties in making the twice-made motion picture, "Once he began to edit it, Woody found that number of speeches were too stagey and too long; that there were many structural problems slowing the action; and that the tension he wanted developed too late. Overall, this is not uncommon; he often rewrites as much as half a movie, as he did on THE PURPLE ROSE OF CAIRO. One thing that necessitates such massive reworking is hi use of long master shots. If a scene is five minutes but a three-second line is wrong, no among of fancy editing can save the entire shot. Also, everything in this film was circumscribed by the set and its playlike quality. Problems that he found such as how the characters were blocked, were as much those of the stage as they were of film. When he saw the first version, eh found he didn't' need some speeches while other things needed to be said that weren't. This is no different than any playwright with a show out of town who reworks the scenes in his hotel room in Philadelphia, except it is more cumbersome and more expensive. As the set was still in place in the Astoria Studios, Woody decided that rather than fiddle with the parts, he'd shoot the whole thing over again. He says now that he'd like to film it a third time." Ironically, SEPTEMBER bears a striking thematic resemblance to INTERIORS in that all its principals are seeking the love and approval of someone else. He did it much better the first time. Allen followed-up SEPTEMBER with another serious effort (and you wonder why Orion has money problems), ANOTHER WOMAN (1988) which although far superior to SEPTEMBER still did not transcend the essential problems which had plagued INTERIORS a decade before and was immediately pegged as bearing eerie similarities to "WILD STRAWBERRIES", another Bergman classic. The characters didn't talk like human beings and the problems the characters faced seemed insignificant and, if not that, certainly blown out of proportion. Gena Rowlands as Marion is unsympathetic as the protagonist devoid of emotion. As she embarks on a spiritual odyssey to discover herself and her desires, we realize we'd rather be out at the popcorn machine watching the butter melt. Gene Hackman has absolutely nothing to do which is a shame since Allen could do for his stalled career what HANNAH did for Michael Caine who would have been stuck doing JAWS 17 - THE BABY if it hadn't been for Allen's jumpstart of his floundering career. Ian Holm is unintentionally hysterical as he mumbles "I accept your condemnation" to everyone who he crosses. ANOTHER WOMAN isn't as painful a film to watch as SEPTEMBER was, but we can still see that Woody isn't quite able to discover the true concerns that make for good drama. In fact, they're the same concerns that make for good comedy, but while Woody is great at pointing out what's funny about our problems, he's not very good at solving them or at least offering some mildly helpful insight through drama. Swedish cinematographer Sven Nykvist does paint pretty pictures though with a camera and again, like Willis work in INTERIORS, that justifies the price of admission alone and David Ogden Stiers playing a young John Houseman once again attests to the brilliant casting talents of Juliet Taylor and her then assistant Ellen Lewis. In NEW YORK STORIES (1989), Allen's heralded and most ballyhooed return to the comedy he had made famous in the early 70's, Allen contributes the third and arguably best installment of this movie trilogy. Scorsese's "Life Lessons" is a winner (let him stick to drama and Allen can handle the comedy) although Coppola's "Life With Zoe" was justifiably panned upon the film's release, perhaps a tad too harshly. Surprisingly, "Oedipus Wrecks", Allen's New York Story isn't as funny as one would expect. He has plumb territory to mine, an overbearing Jewish mother whose upset over the fact he's dating a goy, not a guy, a goy — that's Yiddish for a non-Jew. When he's reached the edge of his rope, she disappears during a magic show. She soon reappears though in the skies above Koch's Manhattan to chastise, advise and embarrass him. He seeks help from a Jewish medium played by Julie Kavner who ultimately returns the appropriately cast Mae Questel to earth. It seems that Allen's years seeking WASP respectability has resulted in a dilution of his ability to parlay his uniquely Jewish experiences into great high comedy. Anyone whose spent their life as the child of a Jewish mother (or grandmother for us youngsters) can tell far funnier stories than Allen in "Oedipus Wrecks". If my grandmother found out I was dating a German woman, she'd poison my kafilta fish. It's still funny enough to be a welcome addition to the Allen filmography. CRIMES & MISDEMEANORS (1989) is Allen's most successful pairing of comedy and drama although it almost seems as if he's making two films with both sides of his personality struggling for dominance (it's okay, we're not talking about matricide). It isn't until the last few minutes of the film that the two stories intersect and its a fairly satisfying conclusion and one of the most compelling (and equally disturbing) analysis Allen has made of human nature and morals. As an ophthalmologist plagued by a lover who won't go away (Angelica Huston), Martin Landau gives a terrific performance finally hiring his brother to see that's she's "gotten rid of". Landau grapples with the moral consequences of his actions for the rest of the film ultimately discarding the belief instilled in him as a child that the "eyes of God are upon us" and embracing a more existential and fatalistic view of the world. Life isn't like the movies, he tells us which is yet another argument why Woody should stop making his dramas that imitate other films. What makes CRIMES so effective and unique in the canon of Allen films is that it does not owe any debt to Allen's coterie of MVP filmmakers (Bergman, Fellini, Renoir, et al), but rather is its own unique work. Similarly, a comedic subplot involving Allen as a struggling documentary filmmaker is darker than any of his previous comedic work and equally powerful —

particularly in its harsh assessment of an egomaniacal television producer appropriately played by Alan Alda who is perfectly cast as a narcissistic, self-important buffoon — "If it bends it's funny, if it breaks it's not". 1990's ALICE is another amusing screen comedy from Allen which doesn't feature the director and while superior to PURPLE ROSE still lacks the comedic punch of his recent dramedies (HANNAH, CRIMES). Allen postulates situations ripe with comic possibilities and fails to avail himself of them in many instances. The scenes in which Mia Farrow as Alice Tate takes Dr. Yang's (Keye Luke) herbs and engages a potential suitor, Joe Mantenga, in a conversation about jazz is just about as funny as this movie gets — which is pretty hysterical, but at the same time Allen's essential premise involving Oriental herbs which can make one turn invisible, super knowledgeable and irresistible seems better suited to comedies of the belly-laugh variety. One can only imagination the long, strange trip Allen would send us sprinting on if his screen persona got ahold of those herbs. If Fielding Mellish or Alvy Singer met Dr. Yang, Elle McPherson would really be in trouble. Nonetheless, ALICE is a sophisticated and intellectually giddy trip through the looking glass well worth making. This time out, like in CAIRO, Farrow is a disenchanted housewife, but instead of being penniless she is a member of the wealthy WASP upper class whose life consists of shopping and an endless variety of gossip. It's tough to buy her conversion to the so-called "good Christian values" which finally send Alice, with kids in tow, off to India to work with Mother Theresa, but her stuttering, neurotic Woody-inspired performance along with those by Alec Baldwin and even sleazy film director James Toback offer sufficient recompense for Allen's creative missteps.

Touchstone attempted to recruit Allen to star in their Bill Murray vehicle WHAT ABOUT BOB? but Allen rejected their overtures. The rival studio had been attempting to lure Allen away from Orion ever since NEW YORK STORIES to little success and ultimately recast the uptight analyst in WHAT ABOUT BOB? with Richard Dreyfuss and found a vehicle for Woody in Paul Mazursky's SCENES FROM A MALL. Allen stayed in front of the camera for this laugh-less concoction from Touchstone managing to make even Allen look stupid in his Armani get-ups. Allen shares the spotlight with Bette Midler (who ridiculously gets top billing) in this inane film in which the couple confesses to a series of infidelities and breaks up and reconciles several times throughout the interminable length of the movie. Allen must of relished the chance to abandon his perpetual nerdy screen image and play a cool Hollywood schmoozer who is lusted for rather than lustful, but the script fails to service the promise of the film. What should be a low-budget, tongue in cheek comedy was instead made as a lumbering, big-budget monster of a film in which Bette and Woody share the screen for two hours feuding in an a recreation of the Beverly Center built in Astoria, New York to suit Allen who refused to shoot in despised Los Angeles. But rather than spoof suburban culture where the mall has become the mecca of contemporary society, SCENES simply focuses on the presumably witty banter between Allen and Midler. This is not to say that SCENES doesn't have its comedic highpoints, it does, but any vehicle which gets Allen out from behind the camera in a full-fledged comedy after 15 years better deliver the

goods which MALL doesn't. I was just waiting for Tony Roberts to do a walk-on to lighten things up, but I was sadly disappointed.

SHADOWS & FOG (1991) is Allen's latest directorial effort, a period piece starring Mia Farrow, Steven Keats and renown thespian Stephen Mendillo.

STARDUST

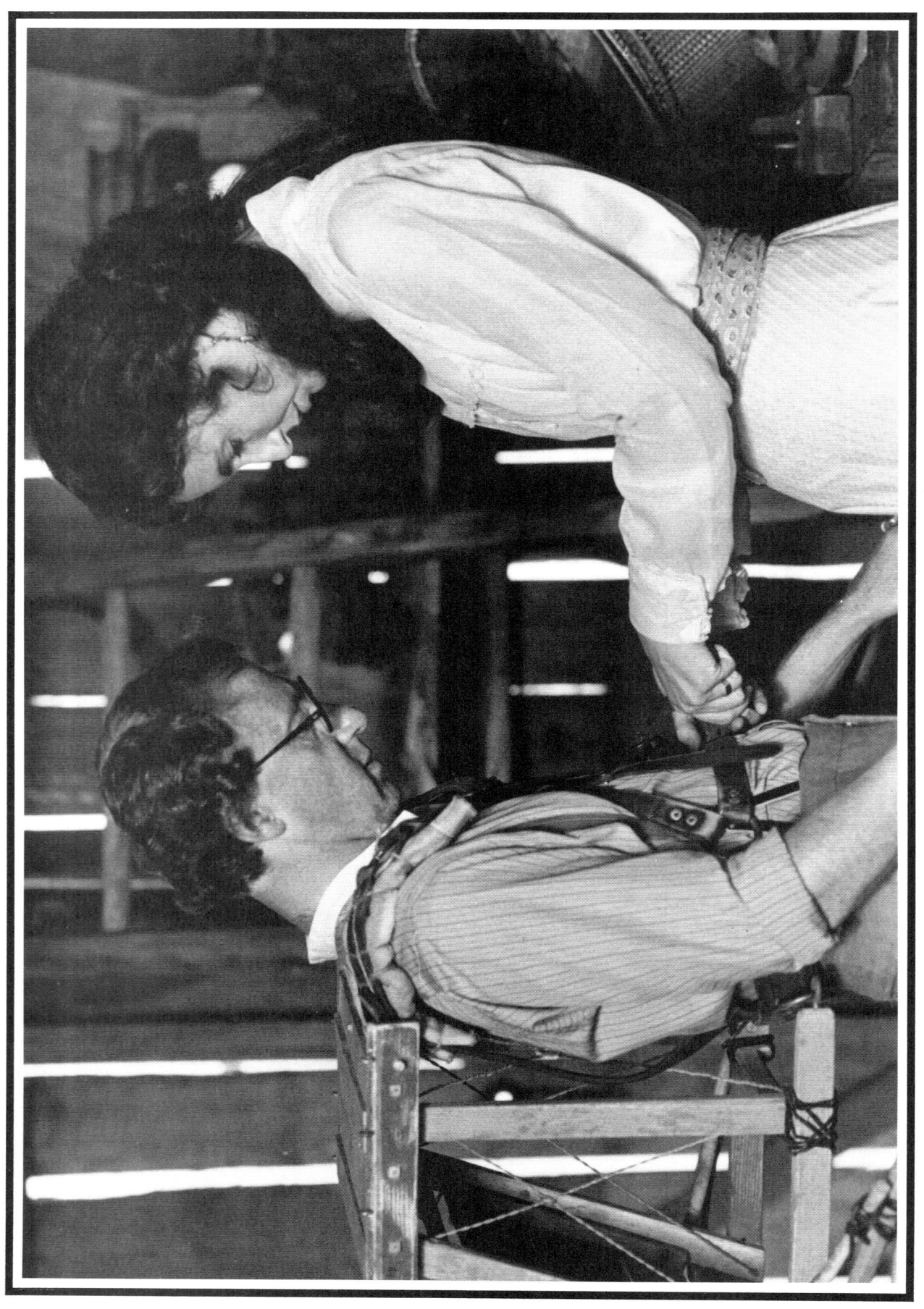

Mary Steenburgen (ADRIAN HOBBS) helps prepare Andrew Hobbs (WOODY ALLEN) for the maiden voyage of his latest invention in A MIDSUMMER NIGHT'S SEX COMEDY

CHAPTER TWO:

"8 1/2 STARDUSTED MEMORIES"

By David Ian Salter

Author's Note: The following discussion of the films *Stardust Memories* by Woody Allen and *8 1/2* by Federico Fellini presumes reader familiarity with the two works discussed. If you haven't yet seen these two films (shame on you!) you should immediately get to a video store and rent them (make sure to get the subtitled version of *8 1/2*, not the execrable dubbed version - it makes a big difference) before proceeding any further into this chapter. Go ahead, I'm not going anywhere.

Now that you've seen both films, we may proceed:

As in other arts, each successive generation of filmmakers has been influenced by the work of the previous generation. It is this process of building upon what has come before that allows an art to flourish and grow. The masters of the 1940s American style of film noir built upon techniques developed by the German Expressionists during the previous decade. Hitchcock was an acknowledged influence on a number of filmmakers who first encountered his films as children, most notably François Truffaut. Perhaps the filmmaker whose influence has spread the furthest is Orson Welles, whose *Citizen Kane* changed much

DAVID IAN SALTER is a well known film critic and filmmaker whose scholarly work on Woody Allen first appeared in the Justice and has subsequently been the topic of much discussion at the USC Film Program in Los Angeles where he is a student. A former Boston native, he currently makes his home in West Hollywood.

that came after. Ironically, this tradition is perhaps one cause of the deplorable state of American film. Modern filmmakers are borrowing the technical advances of earlier films without also building on the soul of those films.

One filmmaker whose body of work does reflect the style and substance of many of cinema's greatest artists is Woody Allen. His cinematic influences are well known, and Allen makes no effort to hide them. He frequently emphasizes his cinematic and literary allusions. Allen is influenced by no previous cinematic figure more than Groucho Marx. Not only is Allen's humor both slapstick and verbal, but there are tributes to Groucho throughout his films. In *Hannah and Her Sisters* Allen's character's life is saved by going to see a Marx Brothers film, *Duck Soup*,. In *Stardust Memories*, when Allen's character Sandy Bates is happiest, the walls of his apartment, which serve as barometers of his mood, (during a particularly hopeless period they are covered by a photograph of an American soldier murdering a Viet Cong) display a larger-than-life photograph of Groucho at his finest.

While the spirit of Groucho pervades in Allen's work, there are a pair of international filmmakers, an Italian and Swede, whose influences are felt more specifically in certain films: Federico Fellini and Ingmar Bergman, both directors whose places in the cinematic hall of fame was long ago ensured.

Allen's love for the works of these two directors was so great that he made a pair of films which were not so much influenced by them as directly inspired by them. Allen's *Stardust Memories* (1980) shares so much in terms of style, theme, characterization and imagery with Fel-

lini's masterpiece *8 1/2* (1963) that it could almost be considered a remake of the earlier film. Precisely the same can be said of Allen's *A Midsummer Night's Sex Comedy* (1982) and Bergman's *Smiles of A Summer Night* (1955). In this case, even the title of Allen's work points up the similarity (with a nod to Shakespeare added for good measure.).

That *Stardust Memories* is Allen's *8 1/2* is immediately apparent from the opening sequence. To begin with, the film is shot in black and white, as is *8 1/2*. This was Allen's second film in a row in black and white: he'd already bucked conventional Hollywood wisdom that black and white is boxoffice poison by making *Manhattan* the previous year. (Interestingly, the only other major American film to spurn color, Martin Scorsese's *Raging Bull*, was released the same year as *Stardust Memories*. Allen remains the only major American filmmaker with the clout to use black and white.) Although *Manhattan* and *Stardust Memories* are both shot in black and white, and although both share the same director of photography, Gordon Willis, the two films have individual looks that are as different as - black and white.

Willis' lighting in *Manhattan* is gentle, making everything it touches look elegant. The lighting here is meant to recapture the glamour and romance of Hollywood white-telephone comedies of the 30s.

Stardust Memories, however, shares with *8 1/2* a very harsh high contrast look which makes places and people look unattractive and grotesque. The details that are so lovingly rendered in *Manhattan* disappear in blobs of light and dark. The white of *Stardust Memories* is almost painful to look at when it comprises most of the image as it does, for example, during the scene on the beach, that in "Jazz Heaven," or the scenes in Sandy's apartment where the blindingly white walls merge into the equally white floor and it is impossible to tell where one ends and the other begins. The whites in *8 1/2* are frequently as bright and featureless, a void similar to the emotional void in the character's lives.

The blacks in *Stardust Memories* (and in *8 1/2*) are frequently just as featureless as the whites. In fact the lighting scheme for much of both films seems heavily influenced by the Hollywood film noir style. Often a character will move from a well-lit area into a pool of darkness where the character is seen in silhouette

Another technique of Allen's which can be traced directly to *8 1/2* is the use of a camera which changes from subjective to objective within the shot. The camera initially shows what Sandy is seeing (the audience is, looking through Sandy's eyes). and suddenly switches to objective (the normal type of shot where the camera is a neutral eye observing Sandy and all the other characters interacting).

Allen uses this device frequently throughout *Stardust Memories*. The first example occurs when Sandy first arrives in his limousine at the hotel Stardust. Fans crowd around his limo and suddenly we are Sandy as the fans speak directly to the camera. As the camera begins to move forward through the crowd, we feel that Sandy has left his car and is moving forward. But there comes a moment when we are no longer Sandy because there he is, entering from screen left and signing autographs as we continue to move forward with him.

Fellini makes sparer use of this technique in *8 1/2*, but there is one instance in which he stretches it to an extreme. It occurs during the cocktail party cum press conference at the foot of the launching pad when Guido is besieged by the press and paparazzi like Sandy was by his fans. The camera adopts Guido's point of view as he moves down the line of reporters, who are all shouting their questions directly into the camera. Suddenly Guido appears walking into the frame in the far background. This shot is particularly jarring because, not only has Guido appeared on screen when we thought we were Guido, but he has appeared so far away that it seems physically impossible that he made it that far back. In contrast, when the camera switches from subjective to objective in Allen's film, he appears on screen near the foreground making it seem possible that he has been walking near the camera all along.

Both Allen and Fellini undercrank the camera in a key scene to simulate the speeded-up, jerky motion of old Mack Sennett silent comedies. Both of them use this technique to distinguish visions from their protagonist's childhood from the many other layers of memories and flashbacks that comprise the films. In *8 1/2* this occurs when the young Guido and his schoolmates play hooky. They visit the corpulent Saraghina and pay her to dance the rhumba for them. The staccato movements of the schoolboys jumping with joy while watching Saraghina and, more obviously, the shot of young Guido being chased around the screen by a Priest from his school, are very reminiscent of a chase scene in a silent film.

Sandy's comparable memory is of a Hebrew school play in which he caused a commotion because he "always resented Abraham being...so willing to kill his son." Here too we have silent movie undercranked action augmented by an old-fashioned iris ending. Certainly references to silent comedies are nothing new to Allen (for example, the slapstick chase in the wheelchair which opens *Sleeper*), but his use of the technique here parallels Fellini exactly.

Allen also borrows certain elements of visual iconography from Fellini. One memorable image in *8 1/2* is young Guido dressed in his Italian schoolboy uniform, of which the most distinctive feature (particularly to audiences in America, where such an outfit is unknown) is a cape. Allen has retained this image and its connection to childhood while reworking its meaning to fit seamlessly into the context and theme of his own film. In *Stardust memories* the young Sandy also wears a cape because as a child he liked to play Superman.

If we follow this element of the cape, the connections to Fellini become increasingly convoluted: the cape is also part of the young Sandy's magician outfit, for magic is at least as strong an element in *Stardust Memories* as it is in *8 1/2*. In visions of his childhood Sandy watches his younger self perform magic tricks as well as fly like Superman. In *8 1/2* the magic act does not occur in the flashbacks to Guido's youth, but in the present form of a demonstration of mind reading by the magician/showman, Maurice, and his partner, the telepath Maya. Even here there is a connection to childhood. Guido's conversation with Maurice reveals that they knew each other before Guido became a famous director, possibly being old childhood friends.

The mystic nature of Maya's telepathic powers (even she does not know how she is able to read minds) brings us back again to *Stardust Memories*, where such mysticism is in abundance among the New Agers who have gathered to greet the aliens landing in a field. Although Sandy's encounter with the aliens can be explained as a hallucination (the spaceships turn out to be hot air balloons), the sequence holds as much meaning for him as the flashback in which Guido's sisters chant the magic words "ASA-NISI-MASA" (the Jungian term "Anima" in an Italian form of Pig Latin or Ubbi-Dubbi) has for the adult Guido.

Although there are stylistic similarities between *Stardust Memories* and *8 1/2*, it is their thematic similarities that mark them as cinematic cousins. To begin with, they are both self-referential films about films. Here *8 1/2* wins the self-referential sweepstakes in that it is a film about itself, that is, the film which Guido is preparing to direct is the actual film we are watching. When Guido's collaborator, the critic Daumier, offers his critique of Guido's script ("And the unexpected appearances of the girl at the fountain...what do they mean?", etc.), he is actually critiquing *8 1/2*, the film in which he himself appears as a character. This sort of ambiguity about the level of reality we are watching (are we watching a film?, a film within a film?, a film about a film? etc.) continues throughout *8 1/2* and is, in fact, never resolved, the ending being as ambiguous as anything it follows.

It is only at the end of *Stardust Memories*, however, that such questions of film vs. reality truly enter the picture. Sure, there are a few shots which begin by appearing to be occurring in the reality of the film, such as the shot of Sandy kissing Dorrie under an umbrella, but then quickly pull back to reveal that we are actually watching a scene from a film within the film (in this case, by using the freeze-frame feature of our VCR to read the slate, we discover that this scene is from a film of Sandy's called *Suppression* - perhaps the *Stardust Memories* version of Allen's *Annie Hall*, which Allen had originally titled *Anhedonia* and which, like *Suppression*, featured the director (Allen=Sandy) and his real-life love interest (Diane Keaton=Dorrie) as the two leads.) With the exception of a few such brief shots, there is never any confusion in Stardust Memories as to whether a scene is one of Sandy's films or not. Never any confusion, that is, until the final sequence, which begins with Sandy and love interest, Isobel, boarding a train. The train looks suspiciously like the one, which opens *Stardust Memories* Sandy begins to describe to Isobel precisely the scene that we are watching on screen (much like Daumier's critiques in *8 1/2*) and then it is revealed that the entirety of *Stardust Memories* has been a film within a film The final images present the audience that has been watching the film at what is apparently a screening for cast and crew.

Here, as with the young Guido's cape, Allen has managed to take a central element of *8 1/2* and re-present it in a similar manner But with its nature and meaning altered. *8 1/2* also ends with a scene in which all of the members of the cast of the film we have just seen, including characters who are supposed to be dead or imaginary, appear en masse. Thus, the structure of the two films is similar. However, the meaning of the two scenes is very different: the gathering of characters in *8 1/2* is meant to convey an amorphous sense of well-being - in effect, life has its share of problems, but that's no reason not to enjoy it. Interestingly, this is the standard message of almost all of Allen's films, most explicitly stated in *Hannah and Her Sisters* as Allen's rationale for not committing suicide. This existential acceptance of life's pleasures in the face of its essential misery is the message of the film within the film in Stardust Memories. Ironically, the final sequence, which is the equivalent of the Allen-esque upbeat ending of *8 1/2*, is actually somewhat downbeat, tempering the earlier uplifting message by allowing the actors in the film to heap criticism after criticism upon the film. The final word belongs to an old man who dismisses the film by saying to his wife with mild disbelief, "From this he makes a living? I like a melodrama, a musical comedy *mit* a plot. But *nisht kein philosofiyeh!* (Yiddish for "But no philosophy!") And the final character to leave the screen is Sandy/Allen casting a rather dejected look at the screen where his latest film (this film) has just been screened. He is obviously disappointed with either the film, the audience reaction, or both.

Sandy turns and slowly walks off screen, and the main lights in the auditorium gradually fade to darkness leaving only two rows of decorative lights on the ceiling of the auditorium visible before the film cuts to black and to the end credits. This is precisely the way 8 1/2 ends, except that it is the younger version of the director (now dressed in a white circus costume negative version of his black school uniform) who is the final character to leave the screen after all of the other characters have left. And once he leaves, as in Allen's film, all of the lights fade out except for a couple of rows of decorative lights surrounding the circus ring. Then these lights pop out and, after a few frames of black, the credits pop on.

Despite all of these surface similarities, Allen's film differs from Fellini's. *8 1/2* is about a film director's search for inspiration. Guido is the leader of a crew that is heavily into pre-production on a big budget film but is failing as a director. He is unable to lead his crew because he has no idea what kind of film he wants to make.and can not make any decisions.

Sandy's problem is different. By the time *Stardust Memories* begins, Sandy has already completed his film. He knows precisely what he wants his art to be. This determination is highlighted by Sandy's anger and frustration when new studio executives reshoot the ending to his film to make it more upbeat. It is worth noting that Guido,who could use some guidance with his latest film (even if it came from dreaded studio executives), never has this problem. Despite an amazing display of incompetence as a director (Guido never actually has the sense of direction required to direct anything until he directs the final scene of *8 1/2*), Guido is granted final cut and complete freedom from studio interference. It is also interesting to note the irony of Sandy's difficulties with the studio in light of Allen's freedom from studio interference .

So, unlike Guido, Sandy is not searching for inspiration, instead he is seeking a validation for his entire existence. How can he justify such a frivolous activity as making movies when people are suffering around the world? Sandy is not particularly pleased with the answer he receives from just about everyone around him (including aliens representing the consensus of the rest of the universe) that his films better the world by making people happy. This is not exactly what a director who is just beginning to make depressing films wants to hear. And Sandy does not necessarily accept this answer to his query. As the film ends, the closest philosophy of

life offered is yet another restatement of the standard Allen viewpoint: life may be full of unpleasantness, but it also provides good moments to savor.And anyway, we don't have a choice in the matter because it's all we've got.

With *Stardust Memories* Allen has taken much of the style, technique, and plot from the work of another filmmaker and has transplanted them, into his own world. There, they have been reformed to serve his own guardedly optimistic message about life. In his very next film, 1982's *A Midsummer Night's Sex Comedy*, he repeated the experiment of closely basing his work on Ingmar Bergman's 1955 film *Smiles of a Summer Night* (*Sommarnattens Leende*). In this case, the process of converting the material into an Allen film was very different. As in *8 1/2*, Allen borrowed a number of elements of the earlier film, but jumbled them up and rearranged them to such an extent that, whereas the correspondences between *Stardust Memories* and *8 1/2* are unmistakable, one must search more carefully for those between *Sex Comedy* and *Summer Night*.

This was neither the first nor the last time Bergman had served as an influence on Allen's work. Allen's serious dramas, beginning with Interiors and continuing through *Another Woman*, have all been accurately described as Bergmanesque. In fact, whenever Allen releases one of these films, one of the things the critics have repeatedly taken him to task for is the perception that by making such films Allen is denying his own voice and trying to adopt that of another (Bergman) in its place, a strategy which never succeeds in art. This is, of course, the same cry of "We like your earlier, funny films" that Sandy/ Allen was so disturbed by in *Stardust*

Memories. Although it wasn't clear in that film whether Sandy was going to heed his fans' (and the aliens') request and return to comedy exclusively, it has since become obvious that Allen himself has not done so, stubbornly insisting on making one serious drama for every two or so comedies.

Although it is not difficult to understand Allen's frustration of critical response to his dramas - most filmmakers like to think of themselves as being capable of more than just one type of filmmaking. It is also readily apparent to anyone who takes a cursory glance at these films (least offensive: *Interiors*, most offensive: *September*) what the critics have been complaining about. There is something so forced about these films, and how could there not be when a director like Allen, whose unique cinematic voice is so clearly tied with a Gordian knot to an American Jewish intellectual sense of humor tries to put on the mask that is most antithetical to everything he is and stands for: that of a super-WASP.

It has long been considered axiomatic that art can only succeed when the artist is completely true to himself. In *Stardust Memories* Allen is not hiding behind the mask of Fellini, but is showing us that of Fellini which is also within himself, and it works. It is probably of no small consequence for the success of the Fellini/Allen artistic marriage that the Jewish sensibility and the Italian sensibility are more alike than almost any two other cultures on earth. However, this is not to say that Allen cannot successfully draw on Bergman as an influence. so long as he does not use Bergman as a stylistic mask, but instead limits the Bergmanesque elements to those which exist within himself. He has done this only once, with limited suc-

cess, in *A Midsummer Night's Sex Comedy*.

It is important to note that in this case, Allen has chosen an atypical Bergman film as his source. Smiles of a Summer Night is the only true comedy from a director widely known for slow, dour films, many of which can best be described as heavy and depressing. Comedy is clearly a field where Allen is the expert and Bergman more of a dabbler,. *Smiles of a Summer Night* is an exceedingly lighthearted and pleasant humanistic comedy of romantic complications among a group of people best exemplified by Jean Renoir's *The Rules of the Game*. (It is of purely trivial interest to note that *Smiles of a Summer Night* was eventually adapted into a Broadway musical and a film, *A Little Night Music*, just as *8 1/2* was made into the Broadway musical *9*.)

In Sex Comedy, Allen has taken the elements from Bergman's film and mixed them into a stew which has even more pieces from Shakespeare's A Midsummer Night's Dream. After the stew has been stirred up and cooked , the original ingredients are not entirely recognizable, and the whole thing tastes more of Allen than of its component influences.

Only the barest outline of Bergman's plot remains. Both films are period pieces set around the turn of the century. Both are about three sets of couples, some or all of whom switch partners by story's end. But whereas only the very climax of Bergman's film consists of a dinner party which brings all of the couples face to face (the servant couple, Petra and Frid are not actually invited guests, but their presence is felt, somewhat), Allen's entire film is, except for the briefest of introductory scenes, comprised of one long such get-together, in this case a weekend at a house in the country at which all three couples are present.

The perfectly schematic nature of Bergman's film, in which all three couples switch partners and never get back to their original partner is muted in Allen's film. Although at some point, it appears that each character will change partners, only two of them do by the end, with one character taken out of the running for reasons of death, one couple remaining together, and one character being left partnerless.

Many elements from Bergman show up combined in new ways. No direct path can be traced from any individual character in Bergman's film to one in Allen's. Allen's characters are amalgams of characteristics taken from two or more of Bergman's characters along with characteristics more typical of other Allen films. Leopold (Jose Ferrer) is fiercely jealous, as is Bergman's Count Malcolm, and, like Malcolm, Leopold appears to attempt the murder of his rival, yet Leopold is also perhaps too old for his young wife, a characteristic, in *Summer Night* of Malcolm's rival, Fredrik Egerman.

Sex Comedy's Maxwell (Tony Roberts) occupies the position as rival to Leopold of his young wife's love held by Henrik Egerman in Bergman's film, yet Maxwell also has much of the lusty, uninhibited, free spirit approach to sexuality embodied in Bergman's coachman, Frid.

A gun and an attempted suicide are elements in both films, but in Allen's film the gun is used for the suicide attempt, while in Bergman's, a noose made from the belt of a robe is used. The gun is used by Malcolm in a game of Russian Roulette to scare his rival for the affections of Desiree Armfeldt.

Mysticism makes its appearance in Sex Comedy, as it did in Stardust Memories. Here the mysticism is in the form of Andrew's (Allen) inventions, a spirit ball which is a sort of mechanical crystal ball. It projects images of the spirit world, as well as the appearance of Leopold's spirit, as a glowing ball after his death. This mysticism and its connection to the forest owes more to the Shakespeare source, but also has its roots in Bergman. At the dinner party in Summer Night, the confrontations begin when the guests drink wine fortified with a drop of a woman's breast milk and a drop of a stallion's seed. This gives it mystic properties causing those who drink it to act uncharacticly . Typical of the way Allen mixes his source elements in Sex Comedy, the mysticism is connected to the spirit ball rather than to wine, but wine does make a passing appearance at dinner in a manner obviously meant to bring to mind Bergman's use of it.

Since *Stardust Memories* and *A Midsummer Night's Sex Comedy*, Allen has not made a film which was obviously inspired by a film of another director. Despite this, the influences of his favorite directors are still discernible in Allen's work, even if one ignores the Bergmanesque dramas which are drenched in the Swedish director's heavy-handed style (and that's precisely what many in Allen's audiences, critics and fans alike, would like to do with these films: ignore them...and hope they go away.) These influences can be detected in elements as subtle but as pervasive as the Felliniesque casting of actors with fascinating rather than beautiful faces in minor roles and as extras. Woody Allen, like François Truffaut, is a director who does not work in a vacuum, but is very conscious and appreciative of the work of those who have gone before him and paved the way for others to follow along the path of cinematic storytelling. Sometimes Allen has strayed from the path by hiding in the shadows of his teachers (mostly Bergman). But when Allen shows that he has learned the lessons of his cinematic mentors, then gone one step further and made them his own, expressing them in his own unique manner and stepping out of their shadows and into his own spotlight, as he did most obviously in Stardust Memories, then his feet are clearly on the path, and he stands revealed as being next in line, worthy of being learned from by those who follow in his steps, just as he has learned from those in whose steps he follows.

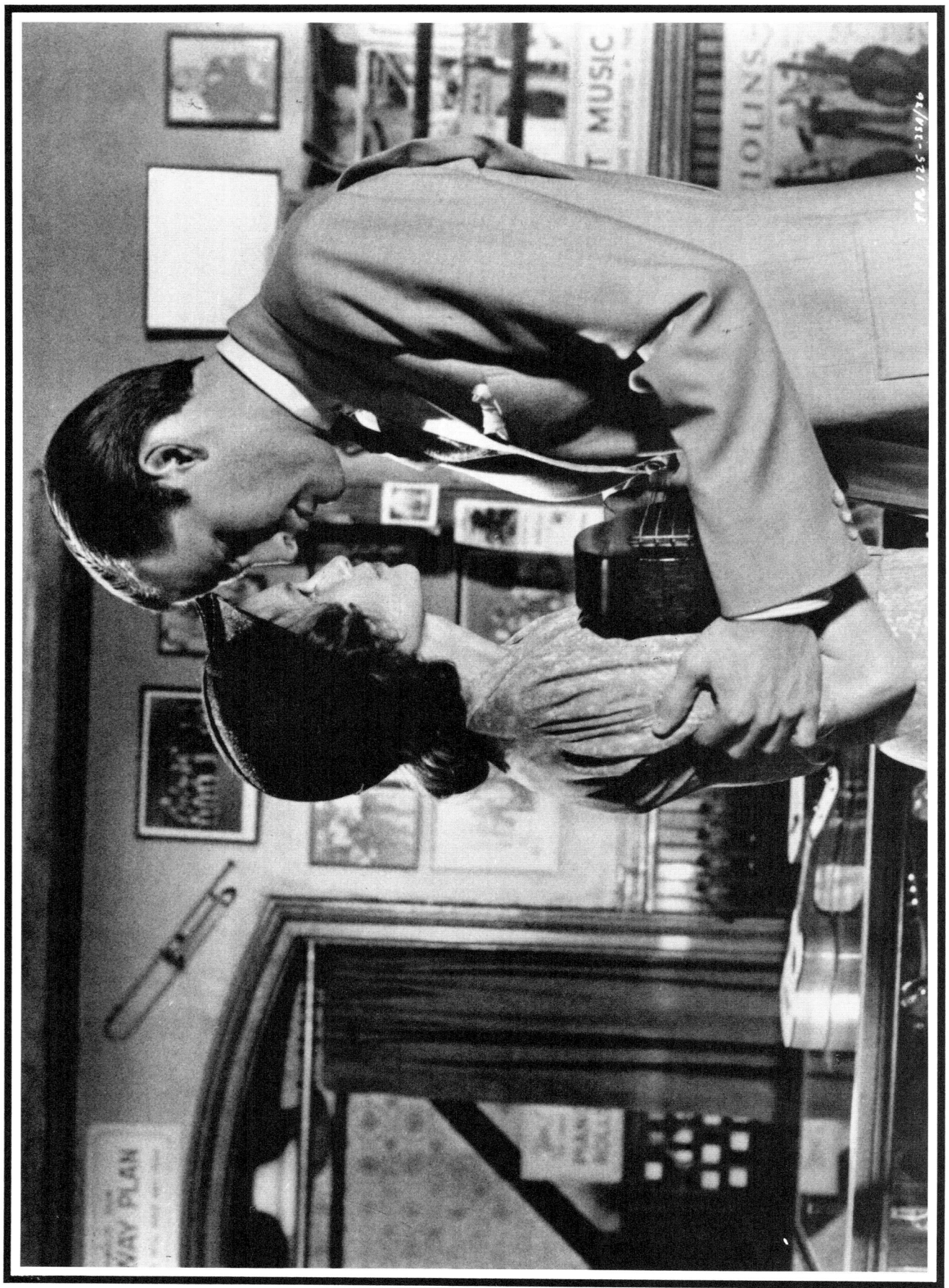

MIA FARROW and JEFF DANIELS emrace in Woody Allen's romantic fantasy
THE PURPLE ROSE OF CARIO"

SEQUELS?

CHAPTER THREE:

"the sequels you never saw (or will)"

By Mark A. Altman

"Right now it's only a notion but I think I can get the money to make it into a concept and later turn it into an idea" - overheard at Tony Lacey's party in *"Annie Hall"*

As we all know, Hollywood has an annoying propensity to clone a good thing. Executives have decided If it did well the first time, it'll do better the second. Did the world really need DIE HARD II, a ridiculous follow-up to one of the greatest action films ever made? Certainly the world would be no worse without MANNEQUIN II: ON THE MOVE or FRIDAY THE 13th - part whatever: JASON MAIMS MISSOURI.

But sometimes there's a film that is made when you really wonder where the characters are once the projector shuts off. Was it really a happy ending, what's Illsa up to these days after leaving Humphrey Bogart at the airport? Woody Allen has certainly had his share of these films leaving stunned audiences gasping as the final credits roll. But we know Woody will never make a sequel. We'll never know whether Hannah and Elliot are still happy, or if Annie and Alvy are back together again? Allen would certainly decry these trivial concerns, after all, the universe is still expanding. Still, I'd like to offer a few of my own thoughts on what would happen if someone turned the projector back on.

Roll 'Em.

SLEEPER 2: JUDGEMENT DAY

Having successfully toppled the totalitarian government of America 200 years after being put into a deep thaw at Roosevelt's Hospital and destroying the leader's nose, the remaining members of the leadership cadre send a killer robot back in time to Greenwich Village to assassinate Miles Monroe before he can change the future and destroy the leader's nose. Stalked by the menacing cyborg played by Nick Apollo Forte of DANNY ROSE fame, Monroe doesn't realize why his area health food store is being attacked by the threatening cyborg. Going to the Jewish Mafia for protection, Monroe falls in love with the don's daughter, Shifka (played by Julie Kavner). The Don is enraged and joins the cyborg on its quest to kill Monroe.

EXTERIORS

In this sequel to INTERIORS, Joey (Mary Beth Hurt), still haunted by thoughts of her dead mother gets a job as a housepainter after being laid off from her job as an advertising copy writer. Michael Keaton plays a down and out movie actor, fired from a major film production for being too contemporary, and steals Hurt away from Sam Waterston who reprises his role as Mike. Joey and Keaton move to a kibbutz in Israel, followed by an enraged Mike, who reveals he is slowly going blind. In America, Flynn (Kristen Griffith) attempts to jump start her floundering film career by doing a nude spread in "Orgasm" which inspires Frederick (Richard Jordan) to write a bestselling novel acclaimed by the New York Times Book Review "as better than anything his wife Renata ever wrote."

In Israel, torn between Mike and Keaton, Joey accidently drowns in the Dead Sea causing her father Arthur (E.G. Marshall) to kill himself. Grief-stricken Mike finds solace in Pearl, Arthur's widow once again played by Maureen Stapleton and the two start a successful tallis repair business .

LONDON

Not hearing from Tracy (Mariel Hemingway) in 10 months, Isaac flies to London where he finds her living in the mansion of popular film actor Donald D. Delilo (Tony Roberts), whose claim to fame is that he is the eighth actor to portray Dr. Who. Isaac tries to convince Tracy to return with him to America, but she refuses and will not go with him to Lecheister Square to see "Grand Illusion". Going himself, Allen meets a beautiful English college professor played by Jenny Augutter (who just broke off a bad affair with David Naughton when he was killed by police in a bizarre accident) and convinces her to come back to New York with him. That night he receives a call at his hotel from Tracy who is crying because Delilo has been offered a feature in Los Angeles with Kim Basinger (Dianne Weist) and is dumping her. She begs Isaac to take her back. Davis flies back with Tracy to New York and realizes that Manhattan isn't as nice as he remembered (David Dinkins cut the sanitation budget) and flies back to London.

MORE
STARDUST MEMORIES

Still in love with Dorrie (Charlotte Rampling) who has recently been freed from a mental institution, Sandy Bates (Woody Allen) flies to Hollywood to save her from starring in a series of Mickey Rourke movies and convinces her to appear in his next serious film. Dorrie plays a talentless screenwriter whose husband just won an Academy Award (the film within a film, October) and she jealously covets his talent. Visiting their summer cottage is her sister played by Mia Farrow. They discuss whether the earth will actually be destroyed by a large meteor. Unhappy with the film, Bates decides to reshoot with another actress (Janet Margolin) and Dorrie goes berserk and shoots everyone. We find out the entire film is being told in flashback by Bates who is actually floating dead in a swimming pool.

The End...I think that's more than enough.

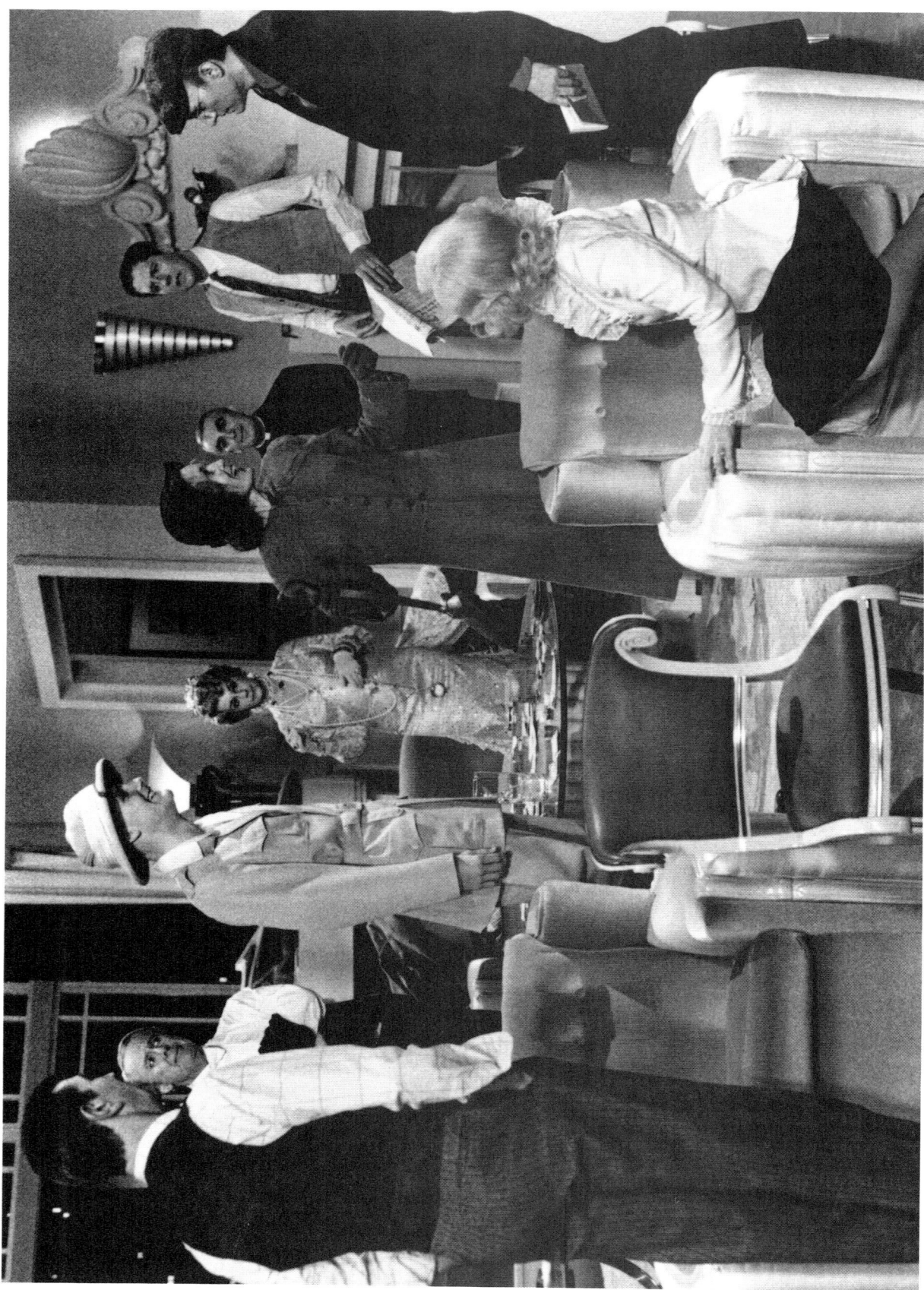

REEL OR REAL?

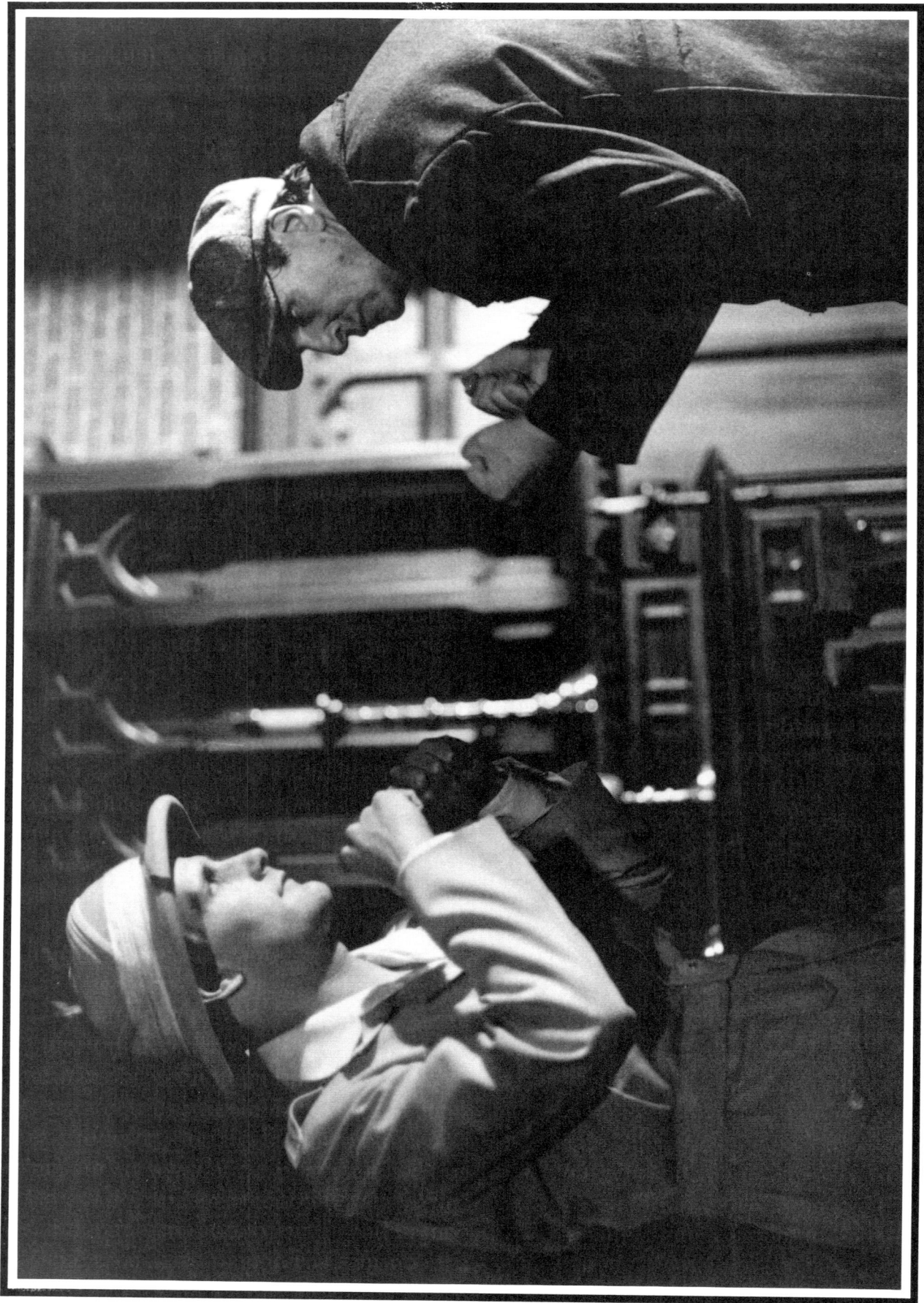

JEFF DANIELS and DANNY AIELLO at odds in "THE PURPLE ROSE OF CAIRO"

CHAPTER FOUR:

"meditating on woody's two worlds: a reel world look at the real world in the purple rose of cairo"

By Thomas Doherty

In SHERLOCK, JR. (1924), Buster Keaton plays a bored projectionist who falls asleep at the switch, strolls down the theatre aisle, and sleepwalks into the action on screen,literally dreaming himself into the movies. Keaton's physical entry into his vision is a luminous metaphor for the psychological immersion of a viewer truly "spellbound in darkness". The imaginative insight found an apt accomplice in the director's technical inventiveness, the groundbreaking achievements in special effects sleight-of-hand he developed for the film's trick shots.

More than half a century later, this silent classic remains the touchstone for the Hollywood on Hollywood "meta-film", the modernist, anxiety of influence movie whose main subject is the medium itself. In America at least, the champion practitioner is Woody Allen. Even more than Allen's oft-spoken affinities for angst and alienation, the connecting thread of his work (visual and linear) has been an obsession with form.

It's difficult to think of a popular convention that Allen has not cheerfully desecrated: spy stories (CASINO ROYALE), gangster bio-pics (TAKE THE MONEY & RUN), SF (SLEEPER), Russian novels (LOVE & DEATH), plus horror, historical drama and "art

THOMAS DOHERTY is a Professor of Cinema and American Studies at Brandeis University. He is a well-known author and contributes to a number of scholarly journals. His analysis of ALICE and THE PURPLE ROSE OF CAIRO are republished from CINEFANTASTIQUE, a magazine for which he is a frequent contributor.

films".With the possible exception of his audacious experiment WHAT'S UP TIGER LILY? (an exercise in pure media mastery if ever there was one), Allen's most elaborate genre-bender is the recent ZELIG, a play-by-play send-up of first, REDS, and second, the whole nature of documentary "truth" and (not incidentally) a chance for the director and his cinematographer, Gordon Willis, to display their technical virtuosity in matters filmic.

"THE PURPLE ROSE OF CAIRO" is a piece with ZELIG showcasing again the imitative talents of Allen's backstage stock company; notably Willis, editor Susan E. Morse, and "period" composer Dick Hyman. Reversing the movement of SHERLOCK, JR. it is a complicated conceit in which function follows form. Cecilia (Mia Farrow) is a put-upon working wife whose only surcease of sorrow is the overripe matinee fare played at the Jewel (a theatre weathering the Depression quite nicely thanks to a menu of escapist tripe with titles like "Dancing Doughboys," and "Broadway Bachelors"). Cecilia takes to a screwball adventure called THE PURPLE ROSE OF CAIRO and its dashing, second male lead, "poet, explorer, adventurer", Tom Baxter (Jeff Daniels), the way Woody Allen of PLAY IT AGAIN, SAM embraced Ingrid Bergman in CASABLANCA.

The feeling is apparently mutual. At Cecilia's fifth viewing, Tom impulsively steps down off the screen and spirits her away. His screen-stranded companions suddenly become characters in search of a player and begin bickering amongst themselves. The movie audience grouse at the all-talk, no action format, justifiably angered that their Hollywood mind candy has turned into an Antoioni film. Mean-

while, back in Hollywood, studio executives get word of the cinematic crisis and dispatch the actor who played Tom, Gil Sheppard (ditto Daniels), to coax his filmic self back into the movie.

The comedic possibilities of the the premise co-exist with-are even subsumed by-Allen's philosophical peregrinations. Like the comedian's early stand-up bits, his New Yorker short stories, and selected dialogue in his movies, THE PURPLE ROSE OF CAIRO is a meditation on metaphysics. The narrative occupies the reel world and the never-never land where worlds collide. The reel world is the ethical and physical universe of classic Hollywood cinema, circa 1935, a place both magical and moral where people are pretty, witty , wealthy and happy — and where anything within the strictures of the Production Code can happen.

As in ZELIG, Allen and Willis labor mightily to recreate the look and feel of the original. Unlike Mel Brooks' hyperbolic homage to James Whale's horror films for Universal in YOUNG FRAKENSTEIN, Allen doesn't so much evoke his models as duplicate them. The film within a film, THE PURPLE ROSE OF CAIRO, is a xerox of an RKO or Paramount Depression era screwball comedy, a master forgery of a production directed by the likes of Lubitsch, La Cava or Sandrich starring Edward Everett Horton or Eugene Pallette, and graced with an Art Deco set (Allen could have pulled off releasing the "reel" PURPLE ROSE OF CAIRO first, on the revival circuit).

Of course the real world according to THE PURPLE ROSE OF CAIRO is a vale of tears. Mia Farrow's born victim waitress is heartrending - preyed on by her husband, society and rude diner patrons. Allen's version of Depression

America has none of the overt artiness of the photographic tableaux in PENNIES FROM HEAVEN. This is a stark and un-stylized landscape (one of the film's tasti-est visual ironies is that the "reel" ROSE - sharply focused, well list, positively glis-tening - looks more lifelike in B&W than the "real" ROSE - dull, dark, washed out - does in color. As Mia's simian mate Monk, Danny Aiello could make Phyllis Schlafly a believer. He's shiftless, brutal, uncaring and unfaithful — and he fights dirty, too. Life with this husband is un-relieved squalor and pain. Once, driven to desperation, Cecilia packs to leave but (so Allen shows us) her only real alternative to domestic terror is prostitution of an-other sort. Clearly, this woman is ripe for a knight from the shimmering screen.

Having established a sure footing in reel and real worlds, Allen plays the ensuing tango fairly straight. His script scores the usual number of wry epigrams ("I just met a wonderful man. He's fictional, but you can't have everything"), but the humor mainly arises from carrying the conceit to its logical lengths: Tom trying to pay for a night out with phony movie money, Tom puzzled when his first kiss with Cecilia doesn't lead to a fade-out ("You make love without fading out?"), and Tom amidst a bevy of hookers in a brothel, in-vincibly ignorant of their function, any-thing forbidden by the Production Code being beyond his ken. All of which is more funny/clever than funny/ha-ha: Al-len's film on film will have no one rolling in the aisles.

This is, in fact, a tragi-comedy with the stress on the prefix. When the reel Tom absconds from the screen, the real Gil seeks out his wayward persona. The actor is soon competing with his character for the affections of their (mutual) biggest fan: Gil pitches woo, sings to Cecilia's ukelele accompaniment (in a particularly lovely musical break), offers to take her away from all this, and, in short, brings a bit of Hollywood to the quiet desperation of her New Jersey existence. Tom re-sponds by taking her on a Keaton-like ex-cursion through his home place, the "reel" ROSE. Her dowdy appearance doesn't mesh with the high-tone gems on screen, but through an expertly re-created "on the town" montage Tom and Cecilia dance away the reels. In the end , she declares herself for Gil, the flesh and blood man. "I have to chose the real world," she tells a crushed Tom.

What happens next is inevitable given the oppositions Allen has set up. Gil splits, leaving sobbing Cecilia to her life of New Jersey hopelessness. It is a cruel ending, all the more so because it seems mandated by thematic, not dramatic ne-cessity. But if, like Cecilia, the audience feels cheated by Gil's betrayal, it is be-cause they, like she, have let motion pic-ture worlds dictate their expectations. Al-len couldn't abide a Hollywood-end on his version of the ROSE, thus de-molishing the scaffolding that holds to-gether his own world view, a view of life expressed by a disbelieving Cecilia as a "movie with no point and no happy end-ing."

In the course of another metafilm, Pres-ton Sturges' SULLIVAN'S TRAVELS, the protagonist, a comedy director with "serious" ambitions, learns that the pleas-ure he gives people with lightweight an-tics is more valuable than the sorrow he lays on them with preachy melodramas. To comedians like Sturges and Keaton, movies were a safe harbor, a happy place for temporary refuge and rejuvenation. For all his love of movies and his facility with film, Allen seems to view the medium as a fraud, a delusion that makes real life all the more miserable by offering a "reel" glimpse of what it might be.

Trapped behind the screen, movie within the movie, cast members MILO O'SHEA, DEBORAH RUSH, JOHN WOOD and EDWARD HERRMANN in "THE PURPLE ROSE OF CAIRO

KAVNER

CHAPTER FIVE:

"a conversation with julie kavner"

By David Ian Salter

Julie Kavner, once best known for her role as Valerie Harper's sister, Brenda Morgenstern on RHODA has since gone onto acclaim Both as the accessory to mayhem on THE TRACY ULLMAN SHOW and as the voice of Marge on THE SIMPSONS and in a series of comedic appearances in Woody Allen's recent work.

In HANNAH AND HER SISTERS, Kavner played Allen's secretary who has to convince him that the ink stains on his shirt are not cancerous tumors. In RADIO DAYS, Kavner had a much larger role as the mother of the family the film centers around and she played the batty medium in Allen's "Oedipus Wrecks" segment of NEW YORK STORIES and Mia Farrow's interior decorator in ALICE.

The first thing noticeable when speaking to Kavner is that although she is from California, she speaks in the same nasal New York Jewish accent that Brenda Morgenstern had. Kavner explains that this is because her parents are from New York. But this is where her resemblance to Brenda ends. Instead, she is extremely friendly and easy to talk to. She lacks the pretentious facade that so many movie actors adopt to distance themselves from the public.

Kavner is a big fan of Woody Allen. Listening to Kavner praise him brings the sense that Woody has been elevated to the role of a deity in her life, an impression strengthened by the say she never refers to Allen by name, but always uses the verbally capitalized pronoun

"He". The last place I came across someone refereed to solely by the masculine pronoun was in the Bible.

She has nothing but praise for Allen, his films, and his directorial technique. "I'm with everybody else, I can't wait to see what he does next. He's got a huge audience who just want to see what he does next. He's so inventive and creative. Who knows?"

Kavner, who is a self-proclaimed film buff, "I love film. I like to talk about film," considers Allen's directorial style second to none. "He choreographs everything, the actors and the camera. The staging and the movement of the actors and the camera are all his. He has a very clear vision of what he wants to see and at the same time he's open to things that might come out in rehearsal and if something doesn't work, he'll change it."

To listen to Kavner describe it, Woody Allen seems to have found the solution to one of the oldest problems of the cinema: How the vision of a sole artists, the auteur, can come out of the collaborative process that is filmmaking taking into account all the input of everyone involved on the set without compromising the director's vision. "I don't mean to say that he squelches any creative input. Not at all! But you're aware of his script, of his vision, what he has in his head, and what he wants the film to be. It is a collaborative process, because he is working with other people. I think that makes a big difference. And it's great. I think it's the best atmosphere to work in."

Many comparisons have been drawn between Neil Simon's play BRIGHTON BEACH MEMOIRS and Allen's RADIO DAYS. Both films do share a common subject, a working class Jewish family in Brooklyn during the forties. But one of the aspects of RADIO DAYS that make it the better film is the portrayal of a Jewish family transcending stereotypes. They all seem like real people, not reel people. Kavner believes that one of the reasons that her portrayal of Mother rings so true is that the family in the film reminded her of her own Jewish family in some ways.

"I'm not very religious myself, but there is something there..Maybe it is what you grow up with or what you pick up. In many movies it's not an issue. In RADIO DAYS, it very much was. This was a Jewish family. I don't think it was a stereotype.

When I was doing it I was not conscious that any of us were stereotypes. I used stuff that I knew from my own family, or things that I heard."

As for Kavner's future with the Woodster, she is hopeful. "I am totally available for the rest of my life. It's in my contract. I know what I want to do which is to be in every movie he makes."

WOODY ALLEN directing MARTIN LANDAU in a scene from "CRIMES AND MISDEMEANORS"

SERIOUSLY

MICHAEL CAINE flirts with BARBARA HERSHEY in "HANNAH AND HER SISTERS"

CHAPTER SIX:

"but seriously...folks"

By Mark A. Altman

"He's pretentious. His filming style is too fancy. His insights are shallow and morbid. I've seen it all before. They try to document their private suffering and fob it off as art" - *a studio executive about Sandy Bates (Woody Allen) in "Stardust Memories"*

"You know, for a guy who makes alot of funny movies, you're kind of a depressive, you know?" - *Daisy (Jessica Harper) to Sandy Bates (Woody Allen) in "Stardust Memories"*

Despite Allen's constant rejoinders that the immortal lines of a fan in STARDUST MEMORIES, "I love your films...especially the early funny ones" was not intended as a barb at the many moviegoers who constantly urge Allen to return to the madcap mayhem of his early films, one has to wonder how he feels by constantly being berated for his attempts to "go serious".

Clearly, Allen is a master of the comic genre. His early films are some of the funniest physical and verbal comedies since the Marx Brothers. And his late-70's romantic comedies are certainly the best work that's ever been done in that genre... serving as the inspiration for a succession of imitators, most effectively the Allen-esque inspired WHEN HARRY MET SALLY.

The problem is the funny Woody of the 60's has given way to the worried Woody of the 90's. Although always neurotic and consumed with questions about death and dying, Allen always kept his tongue firmly placed in cheek until INTERIORS. "It's been such a long time since I made love to a woman I didn't feel inferior to...or am I being tactless," Richard Jordan says to Flynn in that film. In another context, other than a rape scene in one of the most consistently serious films ever made, the line would have been hysterical. Instead, it's just sounds inane and inappropriate.

Allen is constantly saying stupid things like if he was told he could never make another movie, he'd be happy. I'd like to see how happy he is if all the studios decided they weren't going to finance his ventures anymore. Would he really write the Great American novel or would he be holding out a tin can on Madison Avenue to raise money to shoot another feature? Filmmakers who make a film every year are not those I would peg as being miserable. Today, Allen doesn't seem as if he ever enjoys himself but instead lives sequestered in his towering Upper East Side digs away from the real New York. In a recent interview with USA TODAY regarding his commercials for the Italian supermarket chain, COOP, Allen defended himself against charges he was selling out to the establishment. "Let people think what they want," said Allen. "And let's make the truth clear. I don't earn a cent with my films. I have a big family and I thought the offer was interesting."

For $2 million, Allen is directing a series of commercials for COOP, cast by his regular feature casting director, Juliet Taylor. In one spot, aliens land on Earth and ask what is worth eating on the planet. Allen says he's not appearing in the commercials himself because he doesn't feel he'd be credible as an Italian consumer. No, but aliens coming to earth are! For god sakes, this is the man who played an Italian stud two decades ago in EVERYTHING YOU WANTED TO KNOW ABOUT SEX...and that was credible. "I've never been in a supermarket in my life," he said to the press. "There's always a housekeeper who shops for us." And this is coming from the penniless voice of a generation? Fine, do a commercial, you're entitled. But then to feel compelled to justify it by claiming not to make any money, and worse, say that you've never been in a supermarket... how can someone who once had such a keen grasp of the human condition and interpersonal relationships have become so distant from his audience who, for the most part, have been in supermarkets and do not have housekeepers who do their shopping.

It's no wonder his serious films are so dour, Allen has been co-opted by WASP respectability. Having lived with Farrow for ten years now, it seems that Allen has not only given up his disdain for children, but claims to value and love them more than anything featured on the infamous Top 10 Things That Make Life Worth Living list in MANHATTAN (I don't know, Tracy's face is still looking pretty good to me). The issues he tackles that leave the critics and audiences befuddled are now part of Allen's life and the screaming fights of a crowded Brooklyn apartment in Midwood distant memories.

There's a really bad STAR TREK episode called "The Cloud Minders" in which an elite race of beings live in luxury in the clouds while down below the equivalent of THE TIME MACHINE's Morlocks do all their dirty work in the mines keeping the sky city afloat. Apparently, the fans of Woody Allen who chortled for two decades at everything he turned out are bankrolling the new Woody Allen lofty citadel of ideas in which we are not welcome or a part of. No one is saying that we only want to see those early funny films. We're certainly willing to sit by while Allen strives to diversify his output, but to sit idly by and listen to him decry his best works including HANNAH & HER SISTERS and say he feels he never made a really good film is lunacy. Even in ALICE, a fairly amusing little film, Farrow's character is part of uppercrust WASP establishment with nary a Jew in sight. Remember us, Woody? Welcome to the New York Athletic Club. Maybe we'll run into the Berkowitzes hanging on the wall.

The problem as I see it (and Woody you're welcome to tell me I'm wrong) is that Allen dropped out of school and doesn't have his old friends to kvetch with anymore. There's no one to hang out with and talk about the bad old days — the friends for life who are always reminding you about the wild and crazy days of your youth (that inevitably find themselves re-invented through art). Instead of hanging out with the Len Maxwell's and Mickey Rose's who provided such a vital spark for his unique brand of humor in the early days, Allen's going to too many dinner parties and spending much too much time with people who like to talk about Kiekergard and Nietzche. Why doesn't Dick Cavett take Allen out for a night on the town or Tony Roberts sit down and remind Woody that the High Holy Days are coming up and he hasn't written any good Rosh Hashanah jokes recently?

Allen, like Zelig, wants to fit in, but the company he's keeping does not look favorably on an offbeat, witty jokester with a scathing wit and fiery pen. It's better to simply conform then cajole. Allen is trying to come to terms with Mia and the gang and as biographer Eric Lax stated, "...hardly ever tells a joke". Well come on, even if you're not the world's most famous comedian, how can you not joke around...even a little bit. Maybe if he married (or was seeing) a Jewish Julie Kavner type it would revitalize his work. A few Passover's with a Jewish mother-in-law would be enough to get the old Woodster's juices flowing again. But then again, a Jewish mother wouldn't let her daughter have a kid with a guy who lives across the park and isn't married to her...no matter who he is.

But hope springs eternal. In STARDUST MEMORIES, the extraterrestrials told Allen's alter-ego Sandy Bates "to tell funnier jokes" and it seemed as though Allen finally realized that the way to disperse his angst was to do what he was best at and let the Bergmans and Fellinis of the world tell their stories. It was not to be. His jokes didn't get any funnier and his interviews got even frothier.

In HANNAH & HER SISTERS, a soul searching Mickey Sachs (a Woody by any other name) finally realizes, after seeing DUCK SOUP, how much there is to live for. It awakens him to the power of the movies to heel and, at the very least, lift the spirits. That's not any small gift. After all, good comedy is just as valid as good drama? Wrong. We may have all come out of HANNAH thinking that, but clearly Woody didn't.

If only Woody would spend a little more time with the people that he wrote about in the 70's, maybe he would get back on the right track. CRIMES is certainly the best film he's made in the last several years and it best reflects the attitudes which prevailed in his late 70's films coupled with his new post-80's sensibility. It worked...most of the time, even if Judah did spend too much time contemplating the moral fabric of the universe. There was still Alan Alda making an ass of himself and Woody left holding the door as Lester and his love made it to the altar. Now it's time to build on what he did with CRIMES and explore new and interesting stories, but without the brooding, depressive air that typified so many of the serious endeavors he's attempted.

If Woody would just get out of the Park Avenue penthouses and spend a little time munching a hot dog at Nathan's along the boardwalk, I think things would start looking up. There's nothing wrong with spending your nights in tuxes at MOMA (and the Whitney discussing the latest in modern art, what Frank Stella's up to and rebuffing the devastating satirical pieces about the entropy of the Democratic Party. But what about the Woody Allen who sneaks out of a dinner party to watch the Knicks and makes goo-goo noises to Satchel. That's the side of Woody Allen I think we'd all like to see a little more of again.

Maybe he should stop worrying so much about dying, and start worrying about living a little.

BARBARA HERSHEY, MAX VON SYDOW, DANIEL STERN and MICHAEL
CAINE in "HANNAH AND HER SISTERS"

Top: JOE MANTEGA and MIA FARROW
Bottom: MIA FARROW and KEYE LUKE
—Both from Woody Allen's "ALICE"

Top: MIA FARROW
Bottom: WOODY ALLEN directs WILLIAM HURT
both from "ALICE"

CHAPTER SEVEN:

"alice: the new woody's quiet, gentler comedy"

By Thomas Doherty

Known far and wide as the droll diagnostician of urban angst and the last of the high modernists, Woody Allen is also a closet aficionado of bizarro junk and a deft practitioner of the cinefantastique. To take one buoyant example, the "marauding tit" sequence in EVERYTHING YOU WANTED TO NOW ABOUT SEX is the kind of high concept that American International Pictures might have underwritten were Allen's carefree monster-mashing not yoked to a depressing existentialism. "Sleeping with you is a Kafkaesque experience," a groupie tells Alvy Singer in ANNIE HALL, and Allen's version of the fantastic is unnervingly Kafkaesque too - after the fashion of the "Metamorphosis" where everything is perfectly normal, except for that small detail of now being a cockroach.

As the title signals, ALICE is a comedy of manners with a through-the-looking glass perspective. It tumbles head over heels from the level ground of Pnteresque drama to Lewis Carroll flights of fancy (literally so in the case of a soaring levitation over New York's skyline). Though no bummer, the trip is not first class excursion. Against the solid nourishment of his last two entrees; HANNAH AND HER SISTER or CRIMES AND MISDEMEANORS, ALICE is slight Allen. Rank it somewhere between RADIO DAYS and about level with the "Oedipus Wrecks" chapter of NEW YORK STORIES.

No crowded ensemble effort, ALICE is a one-woman show. A mad-hatted Mia Farrow plays a mousy Park Avenue housewife unfulfilled by the daily grind of manicures, massages and shopping. WASPy husband, William Hurt, is insensitive and oblivious to her percolating discontent Her so-called friends are airhead gossips,and her children a background buzz. Enter handsome saxophone player Joe Mantegna, who gallantly retrieves her volume of Edna St. Vincent Millay. The couple's eye-line matches. Already beset by psychosomatic back pains, Alice now has butterflies in her stomach.

As in GREMLINS, oddly enough, what lifts the dreary occidentals out of their mundane existence is the injection of some oriental mystery - and it is again the venerably Keye Luke (in his final role, sad to say) who plays the dispenser of Chinese aphorisms and supernatural trouble. Like the "Eat Me/Drink Me" bottles imbibed by her namesake, his herbal potions transport Alice into a wonderland where relief - and invisibility, human flight and sexual magnetism - is just a sip away.

Embarking on her first extra-marital affair, Alice is herself a bottled up Victorian - frustrated desire, killer guilt, and painful self-consciousness ("I've been meaning to go on a diet," she blurts right before the lights go down). Her first herb induced personality transformation is a revelation. In the blink of an eye, in a close-up long take encounter with Mantegna, she blossoms into an accomplished flirt and moistly draws in her prey.

As the herbs continue to kick in and escalate in outlandish effect, the film loses its own equilibrium. The tone shifts in a menage of styles - marital woes and confessional self-discovery set aside whimsical bouts of invisibility and bluescreen-wrought human flight - are designed to produce a delightful magical ride, not a queasy motion sickness. The film's pat-

ently off-kilter landscape doesn't smooth things out. Though nominally set in the '90's and punctuated by timely lines ("Watch Good Morning America," her inattentive husband advises), the vaguely Art Deco set design is a retro=displacement and the costuming might have been lifted whole cloth from THE PURPLE ROSE OF CAIRO.

By setting ALICE both in and out of the real New York, Allen means to anchor the tale in a reality sturdy enough to sustain the drama, but unsteady enough to support the hallucinatory. In the past, Allen's detours into the unreal have been mainly cinematic - Alvy Singer dragging Marshall McLuhan into the frame in ANNIE HALL, Jeff Daniels walking out of the screen in THE PURPLE ROSE OF CAIRO and the whole of ZELIG. Under his skeptical eye, trick photography exposes the lying image in the age of computer graphics. In ALICE the transparently unspecial special effects don't break down the cinematic frame; they break up the nature of the narrative and the flighty whimsy falls to earth.

The cliched plot is a disaster, WHAT'S UP TIGER LILY? - before the English language dubbing - was more compelling. A bored housewife trapped in a loveless marriage and a dollhouse of her own making? And what decade is this anyway? And what social stratum for that matter. The spiritual trouble of the idle rich is not exactly a natural hook for mass audience identification. Allen's earlier New York films were about folks at the lower and middle rungs of the social ladder - marginal artists, academics, and struggling whatevers. From the low rent TAKE THE MONEY AND RUN to the luxury interiors of CRIMES AND MISDEMEANORS is a major shift in class allegiance. ALICE takes in the filthy rich ambiance to (apparently straight faced) extremes. With her limo drivers, cooks, attendants, and babysitters, Alice has more back-up assistance than MC Hammer. One reasons the New York of ALICE, for all the "on location" shooting seems so unreal is that Allen plainly has not taken the subway lately.

Allen enthusiasts can divert themselves by cataloging moments from his past - a funny drug sequence reminiscent of the huddle around the Orb in SLEEPER, Bernadette Peter's as a writer's muse and Alec Baldwin as an old boyfriend doing apparitional turns that recall the Humphrey Bogart companionship of PLAY IT AGAIN, SAM - but ALICE is a radical departure from traditional Allen territory in one major way: religion. The director who made neurotic New York Jewishness a culture-wide malady switches religious affiliations. Alice is a former "good Catholic" girl and would-be nun who is not as lapsed as she things. But as in CRIMES AND MISDEMEANORS, the first film in which Allen took his Jewish heritage more as a lifeline than a punchline, the director treats Catholicism seriously. In the case of the film's literal patron saint, none other than Mother Theresa herself, he is downright reverent. In BANANAS and HANNAH AND HER SISTERS, Catholic ritual was a source of wild hilarity - hawking cigarettes from the communion rail, studying a catechism with mayonnaise and white bread. On the evidence of ALICE, Allen is a lapsed infidel. This is the first Allen film that would leave viewers open-mouthed and disbelieving at the finale. Can the religious skeptic be serious about the redemptive worth of a life of nun-like devotion and self-imposed vows of poverty? Go ask Allen.

.....IN PARIS

CHAPTER EIGHT:

"a jewish dental student in paris"

*By Mitchell Rubinstei*n

I am the only person in the city of New York who has not met Woody Allen. Everyone else around here has met him. Bumping into Woody is a sort of badge of legitimacy for New Yorkers, and anyone who admits he hasn't is regarded as a second class citizen; sort of a tourist from Iowa who just stepped off the train and doesn't know his way around. A perusal of your average Upper East Side cocktail party will reveal that 39% of those in attendance stood behind Woody on line at the Carnegie Delicatessen. 25% will say they were standing on the corner of 75th and Central Park West when Woody and Mia pulled up in a cab, while 21% will swear he was with Diane Keaton and it was the corner of 46th and Broadway. Woody takes lots of cabs. The remaining 15% will invariably have creative stories of bumping into Woody at book stores, concerts, plays, and of course, Michael's Pub (Where he sits in playing clarinet with the band Monday nights). Having been forced to sit through many of these stories myself I have often wondered about New York City's almost maniacal devotion to a most unusual pop icon.

The proprietary feeling of New Yorkers for their hero is understandable. Woody loves the Big Apple as well. He lives there and has immortalized many of its virtues and faults on

MITCHELL RUBINSTEIN *has written extensively on subjects in music, film and television. This is one of a series of essays written while he was backpacking through Europe. He and his cat live in Philadelphia but hope to correct that as soon as possible.*

film. In a way it seems only fitting that the Prince Valiant of Manhattan Island is a short, nearsighted, Jewish intellectual, whose insight and wit simultaneously applaud and condemn religion, ethnicity, politics, education, the arts and just about anything else people argue about at cocktail parties.

He's a comedic philosopher who dissects humanity and human failings of every kind, and who holds our darkest fears up for all to see, somehow managing to make us laugh at it all.

But is there really anything particularly "New Yorkish" about the man's writing? On the surface of course there is. The city is the setting for nearly all of his films. One of them, MANHATTAN, even bears the name of New York's most famous borough. But the substance of Woody Allen's writing must have a broader reach than that, otherwise his movies would not be such popular phenomena. Fans in one city alone do not an auteur make. What kind of life does Woody's material live outside New York? Way outside, I mean.

They love Woody in France too. I know this because I was there recently and I had an opportunity to experience what I can only call "Woody abroad".

Movies were not high on my list of things to do when I visited Paris last summer. My primary intention was to become one of the million or so nameless foreigners who flocked to the various sights and adventures of the city on the Seine. As it turned out, the people I met there provided me with far more entertainment than the numerous and thoroughly deflowered tourist traps of the Champs Elysées.

My guides in the city were a pair of students from the southern part of the France (Nice, to be exact). We traveled together for about two weeks, having met at a hostel in Toulouse. Paris was our common destination. I of course had never been there and found myself quite relieved to have a couple of natives to show me around. When we arrived my companions decided it was up to them to educate this poor provincial in the ways of the Grande Ville de Europe. They showed me around in style, for the most part avoiding the summer hordes. I had not anticipated though, that one of our chief diversions would be something entirely different from the usual Eiffel Tower, Louvre, Arc de Triomphe whirlwind package tour . Something, in fact, that I associated more with New York, with home, than anything else I did over there.

Martin and Robert, or Marty and Bobby as I would call them in my thickest New York accent, were real movie buffs. I found this out my first night in Toulouse when they killed me in movie trivia. (It's also how I found out that James Horner wrote the score to WOLFEN). They were crazy about American films and were thrilled at the prospect of going to see one with an honest to goodness American. Actually, Europeans in general share a far greater fascination with the films of Hollywood than we Americans do with European made films. For me, knowing that the United States is the movie capital of the world is not at all the same thing as seeing that dominance up close. It may in fact be the only thing our country has left to be admired for. What I had not realized, is the incredible abundance of genuine Made in U.S.A. celluloid that floats around the city of Paris at any given time, and especially during the summer.

Paris is thick with cinemas of every description. Big ones, little ones, fancy ones, dirty ones, whatever. It is not just dominated by thirty screen movie space arcs like many cities here in the U.S. Just picking up a copy of the Pariscope (A kind of Parisian Village Voice) will reveal several dozen American films at least. Some new, and some which have not played in the states in years. The ones marked "V.O.,or "version originale" have the original English dialogue with french subtitles. Reading the listings is almost like going to the video store. In one issue I found adds for Star Wars, Angel Heart, The Sting, and Chinatown...all playing at various smokey little cinemas on the Left Bank. During lunch on our third day in the city, Martin, Robert and I sat with a copy of the Pariscope, looking for a suitable movie for that evening. As the American in residence it was up to me to pick which one, but they could not resist reading over my shoulder and pointing out various options.

I discovered that Martin and Robert's favorite actors included Clint Eastwood, Robert Redford, Harrison Ford and of course, Kim Basinger and Michelle Pfeifer. I think they liked action movies because such films cross the language barrier fairly easily. Comedies, so my friend Martin felt, rely more on the intricacies of a particular language than adventure films and loose quite a bit when translated. I did not agree completely, though I had to admit it was an interesting thought, especially for a guy who had never had a chance to watch Siskel and Ebert. Then, at the bottom of the listings page, I saw a French word I thought I recognized but I was not sure. I pointed it out to Robert who looked at it and said SLEEPER.

SLEEPER? I told them it was a comedy by Woody Allen and they were immediately intrigued. They had heard of Woody of course and could name his more pop-

ular films but neither of them had ever seen any. I resisted the urge to tell them the story of how I stood on line behind Woody at the Carnegie Deli. Their impression of him seemed to be that of a sort of American Ingmar Bergman. In other words, they felt his films probably were very artsy and creative but were also probably too mysterious and convoluted for them to understand or enjoy. SLEEPER? Hmmmm. These two didn't know it yet but they were in for quite a shock.

I had time to build them up for it. The show didn't start until nine thirty and we weren't even finished with lunch yet. By dinnertime I had them convinced we were going to see a dark and critical political comedy about a man facing his future and his society's degeneration into totalitarianism. "You'll love it," I told them, "trust me." They were a bit intimidated.

I had made no mention of Woody Allen kidnapping a nose, flying in a giant balloon suit, hanging out a window suspended by magnetic tape or eating a banana the size of a Buick with Diane Keaton. I figured if they were not expecting it, the shear lunacy of SLEEPER would take them more by surprise and have more impact. Sadly though, it did not go quite as I planned. While waiting on line for tickets there were plenty of people who had seen it before, and Martin and Robert overheard enough bits of conversation to realize that they'd been had.

We sat through the whole thing and they did laugh at the right times, though it was not quite the thundering reaction I expected. There was no screaming with laughter to the point of hyperventilation. I began wondering if I had made such a good call after all. In fact, from the moment I saw the ad in the Pariscope I had been so singleminded in my efforts to get them to see it, that I had not taken into account the fact that they might (gasp) not like it. Of course, my friends might have enjoyed it but simply found it less funny than I did. The entire audience in fact seemed somewhat more subdued than American audience with whom I had first seen the film. I was a bit apprehensive, as I had given them such a buildup for it. Such responsibility. Perhaps they found it tasteless and asinine. Would I now and for the rest of their lives be to them that typical bawdy knave of an American with no taste and a laugh like a maimed hyena?

I thought briefly about Neil Murray, an exchange student from England who had stayed with the family of a friend of mine when we were back in high school. As it turned out, one of the local television stations ran episodes of "The Benny Hill Show" every evening and Neil never missed it. I was over there one night and listened carefully as he tried explain why this man was considered funny, and why legions of British followers swear he is the funniest man who ever lived. I had no problem with his explanation. The problem was that I found Benny Hill not only unfunny, but dare I say it, tasteless and asinine. Well I did dare to say it and Neil was about as shocked as can be. He was too amazed to be offended. I think he actually felt sorry for me, I guess sort of the way I would feel about someone who didn't like Woody Allen. I should add that I do know Americans who find Benny Hill very amusing, but I've found it to be the exception rather than the rule.

This is what was occupying my thoughts as I sat through the film, not enjoying it quite as much as I should have been. That my devotion to this film might be as inexplicable to Martin and Robert as Neil's Benny Hill idolatry had been to me. There

were a few things in my favor however. One is that comedy reflects society. Since Americans (myself included) are, in general, woefully ignorant of the workings of European societies, it is not hard to see that we have trouble with their humor. American popular culture on the other hand, especially now, has become sort of a de facto world standard (a fact to which I attach little real value). I found many people during my trip who were surprisingly well versed in the ways of our rock stars, our movie stars, even our video games. With this in mind it seemed reasonable to hope that my friends might be more adaptable than I had been as a youngster.

I won't leave you in suspense, though you could probably have guessed anyway. Martin and Robert loved the film and almost talked me into seeing it a second time. They explained that they just were not used to getting as wild as I described American audiences. Culture shock. Martin wondered how I could hear all the jokes while I was laughing so hard. It is a rare comedy indeed that can make me laugh out loud the fifth time I see it, and I told him so. I believe the only other movies which could claim the honor would be A NIGHT AT THE OPERA and maybe BLAZING SADDLES.

My friends seemed to have no problem understanding either the subtle or the gross in Woody's humor. It was interesting though how they seemed more absorbed by Woody's political and social jabs than they were by his slapstick routines. Robert felt that much of the film poked fun at the belief that the future will hold the solutions to all our problems, and that by developing science and technology we can overcome our myriad societal shortcomings. It was not a bad analysis.

After all, what manner of genius would it take to hide something important in a package as conspicuously silly as SLEEPER? Did he even realize it as he was writing it? Who knows. What would happen if I were to take them to see TAKE THE MONEY & RUN, or BANANAS? I am normally cautious to avoid over analyzing films. It is always too easy to find meaning and symbolism that the writer probably never thought of.

When traveling in Europe you will find that the natives are often more educated in United States affairs than your average American, which is hardly surprising considering the education of your average American. That night back at the hostel the three of us, along with a few other students from other parts of Europe, had a rather interesting discussion about the past and probable future of the United States. Though I was hardly able to recall more than an embarrassingly small portion of French politics, I found that these French and German kids, only one of whom had ever been in the United States were talking very eloquently about what they called its social ills and economic downfall. I fought down a sudden rise of patriotism and forced myself to listen. It was an extremely rare opportunity to be completely immersed in Europeanism.

The best part came when one German girl mentioned an American film she saw when she was in high school. She described it as a comedic documentary about a fictional man who takes on the physical and psychological characteristics of everyone he meets. He is viewed as a sort of circus freak and is both celebrated and ostracized by the rest of society. She remembered the film as intelligent and extremely humorous, but also very biting in its satire. She could not for the life of her

remember the name of the film or the film maker, but she remembered being very surprised that the writer was an American. As soon as she described it I realized she was talking about none other than ZELIG, written and directed by Mr. Woody Allen. I said nothing. Martin and Robert didn't know the movie she was talking about. It was a funny moment for me. On the one hand were two Frenchmen who knew that ANNIE HALL had won best picture in 1977, but until several hours earlier had never actually seen a Woody Allen film. On the other was a German girl who remembered the film ZELIG in detail but couldn't remember who had made it.

For the moment I decided to just keep quiet. The film, as she described it, was a parody of the American's embarrassment over the decline of his culture and his desire to regain the acceptance of the others whom he has wronged. She pointed out those scenes where Leonard Zelig took on the appearance of a Black man and again when he became an Asian. These, she said, show guilt over our society's treatment of minorities. It was amazing, she said, how it was possible for a film to deal with such serious subjects and at the same time be so hysterically funny. She felt this showed the writer to be a more penetrating thinker than one who could deal with such things only seriously. This might have been one of those moments of over analysis, but I found myself agreeing with her. To a point, that is. I was not about to make the generalization that comedy patterned on serious subjects is necessarily inspired by serious underlying motives. After all in History of the World Part I, Mel Brooks wrote a Las Vegas-like dance number on the subject of the Spanish Inquisition. I found it to be very funny but I never got the impression that Brooks was doing any particularly deep thinking when he created it. It certainly inspired no deep thinking on my part. Never having spent much effort prying into the nature of comedy, I wondered just how important it really is to know why a writer is joking about a particular subject. If it makes you laugh, then it's funny. If a person got something different out of the movie than I had, so be it.

Anyway, it became a recurring theme as Martin, Robert and I went out to several more films, including one more by Woody Allen (for the record, STAR-DUST MEMORIES on a double bill with 8 1/2). We would go out for drinks afterward and conduct sort of a postmortem on each movie, usually reading a bit more into each one than I felt justified in doing. And when they would ask why I thought my opinion was valid and theirs were not, what was I to say? Is it wrong for me to assume that I know more about Woody Allen simply because I'm from New York? If I ever run into him at Elaine's maybe I'll ask him — not that a poor dental student like me could afford a meal at his bistro of choice. But then, who would believe me anyway?

SLY—WE'RE SURPRISED! Sylvester Stallone accosts a helpless woman in "BANANAS". Rocky would be disappointed.

ENCYCLOPEDIA

2173

Year Fielding Mellish (Woody Allen) is awakened in "Sleeper"

29485

Virgil Starkwell is branded with this number when incarcerated after an attempted robbery in "Take The Money & Run".

621-4598

If you want to reach Dick Christie (Tony Roberts), this probably isn't the number to call —it's his home.

ABEL, JACK (John Rothman)

Blabbermouth from Columbia, asks Sandy Bates (Woody Allen) to guest lecture in his screenwriting class in "Stardust Memories".

ABIGAIL ADAMS

While touring New York in "Hannah & Her Sisters", Holly is introduced to this landmark of Manhattan architecture by David (Sam Waterston).

ABRAHAM, JERRY (Bob Maroff)

Sandy runs into an old friend from Flatbush who drives a taxi while reliving his "Stardust Memories" at a film culture weekend.

ACADEMY OF MUSIC & DRAMATIC ARTS

Tracy (Mariel Hemingway) is accepted to attend the prestigious acting academy in London which Ike (Woody Allen) at first encourages her to do and then tries to discourage her from going.

ACADEMY OF THE OVERATED

Gustav Mahler, Isak Dinesen, Carl Jung, F. Scott Fitzgerlad, Lenny Bruce, Norman Mailer, Walt Whitman, Heinrich Boll, Van Gogh, Ingmar Bergman. Mary Wilke (Diane Keaton) and Yale's (Michael Murphy) pretentious list of overrated artists arouses the ire of Isaac (Woody Allen) in "Manhattan". Incredibly, Mailer hadn't even directed "Tough Guys Don't Dance" yet and still made it on.

ACKERMAN, IVAN

Alvy's elementary school classmate in "Annie Hall" who always had the wrong answer, 7 plus 3 equals 9.

ADVANCED SEXUAL POSITION & HOW TO ACHIEVE THEM WITHOUT LAUGHING

Victor Shakopolis' bestselling book in "Everything You Wanted To Know About Sex".

AJAX WIDGET COMPANY

The company Joe Green is employed by in "Take The Money And Run".

"California, Max...let's get the hell outta this crazy city - we move to sunny L.A. All of show business is out there."
— Rob (Tony Roberts) to Alvy in "Annie Hall"

ALICE (1990)

Directed by Woody Allen, Alice is the story of unhappy housewife Alice Tait (Mia Farrow) who when given magical herbs discovers a lot more about herself and the world she lives in.

ALLEN, WOODY

B: Dec. 1, 1935. Born: Allen Stewart Konigsberg. Director, Writer, Comedian, Professional Neurotic.

ALMA

Lester (Alan Alda) promises to put her in a television show although he's not sure what part she'd be right for...and he's just bought a new casting couch in "Crimes & Misdemeanors".

AMES, CHARLOTTE (Gabrielle Strasun)

Actress played Sandy Bates' mom in previous film he directed she tells him when sees him in "Stardust Memories". Remarking on how young she looks, she tells him about all the nipping and tucking she's had to retain her girlish figure.

AMILLIO, GENERAL

Introducing the new dicator of San Marcos in "Bananas"

"Can you imagine the level of a mind that watches wrestling"
— Frederick in "Hannah & Her Sisters"

ANAHEDIA

The original title for "Annie Hall", the psychological term for someone who can't enjoy themselves.

ANDRESS, URSULA

Introduced in "Casino Royale" as "a personal friend of James Bond". Starred in both "What's New Pussycat" and "Casino Royale" with Allen. Best known for playing Honeycomb Rider in "Dr. No", the first James Bond film and giving new meaning to the words small, white bikini.

ANGELINA

The fortune teller Tina Vitale (Mia Farrow) consults in "Broadway Danny Rose" to see what she should do about her lover Lou (Danny Apollo Forte).

APPLEBAUM, SIDNEY

An ill-fated plotter attempting to kill Napoleon and take over France for himself. He would not succeed in "Love & Death" or in Life & History.

ARIES PROJECT

The top-secret operation to clone the dead Leader's nose in "Sleeper".

ARMSTRONG, A.D.

Wanted for many crimes including marrying a horse by the authorities in "Take the Money And Run".

"If God is testing us, why doesn't he give us a written"
— Boris about to go into battle in "Love & Death"

ARTURO (Eugene Anthony)

The maitre d' in a chic Manhattan club, one of the supporting players in the fictional Purple Rose of Cairo film playing at the Jewel in "The Purple Rose Of Cairo".

ASHCROFT, TEDDY

Nerdy exterminator, Jane introduces to Cecilia (Mia Farrow) in "The Purple Rose of Cairo".

AUNT TESSIE (Rashel Novikoff)

They say she was a great beauty, the one with personality. She was a great dancer, just take a look at "Annie Hall".

BACHARACH, SID

High-powered entertainment manager who steals Lou away from Danny Rose at the urging of Tina Canova in "Broadway Danny Rose". No relation to Burt. He's no Connie DeNave.

BACHRACH, BURT

Provided the scores to "Casino Royale" and "What's New Pussycat".

BAKER, JOSEPHINE

Dances at the Folies Bergere where she does Chamelon in "Zelig"

"This is shaping up like a Noel Coward play. Somebody should go out and make some martinis."
— Isaac after finding out Mary has started seeing Yale again in "Manhattan"

BANANAS (1971)

Directed by Allen, the story of a banana republic and how it's changed by one man, Fielding Mellish.

BARBARA

Woody's sister in "Crimes & Misdeamenors" who is tied up and defecated on by man she met in Personals. There's a motto in this for all you New York Magazine readers.

BARDEBEDIAN, HERMAN

Gil Shepherd's real name in "The Purple Rose of Cairo" who played adventurer Tom Baxter.

BARRY, JACK

Host of "What's my Peversion" in "Everything You Wanted To Know About Sex"

BATES, SANDY (Woody Allen)

Hounded filmmaker played by Woody Allen in "Starudst Memories".

BAUMEL, CHAIM RABBI (Baruch Lumet)

After writing in to "What's My Perversion" in "Everything You Wanted To Know About Sex", Rabbi Chaim gets to be tied up and spanked by a model while watching his wife eat pork as part of his dream fettish.

"Did you grow up in a Norman Rockwell painting"
— Alvy asks Annie when she mentions Grammy Hall in "Annie Hall"

BAXTER, TOM (Jeff Daniels)

High-adventurer/explorer played by Gil Shepherd (Jeff Daniels) in "The Purple Rose Of Cairo"

BECK, JACKSON

Narrator who spins the terrifying tale of Virgil Starkwell in "Take The Money & Run"

BELLOW, SAUL

Sheds some light on Zelig's condition in "Zelig".

BEN (Sam Waterston)

Moralistic rabbi going blind in "Crimes & Misdemeanors"

BERGICOV

Village idiot going to village idiot convention in Minsk.

BERGMAN, INGMAR

Why would he be in a book about Woody Allen? Typo?

BERKIE'S PET'S

Local pet shop Virgil attempts to rob in order to support himself in "Take The Money & Run", but is undone by the prescence of a large, menacing gorilla.

"If the Gestapo would take away your Bloomingdale's charge card, you'd tell 'em everything"
— Alvy to Annie in "Annie Hall"

BERLE, MILTON

Uncle Miltie sees Lou Canova in "Broadway Danny Rose" at the Waldorf where Canova is making his comeback. Berle is joined by sports commentator Howard Cosell.

BERNSTEIN, NAT

Died at 37 of amyothrophic lateral sclerosis in "Stardust Memories." A friend of Sandy's from the neighborhood in Brooklyn, once again reminds him about mortality and the eventuality that we will all die.

BERNSTEIN, WALTER

Blacklisted writer who was blackballed from the industry in 1950 during the HUAC investigations portrayed Annie's date in "Annie Hall" when she bumps into Alvy at "The Sorrow and The Pity". Also appeared in "The Front"

BETTELHEIM, BRUCE

Psychoanalyst who comments on white room studies of Zelig in "Zelig".

BIERBAUER, TED (Theodore R. Smits)

Writer for NY Daily Mirror in Allen's fictitious mock-documentary "Zelig".

BILL

Writes jazz heaven scene for the studio in "Stardust Memories" to the disgust of Sandy.

"To me nature is, I don't know, spiders, nature and bugs and big fish eating little fish and plants eating plants...it's like an enormous restaurant"
— Boris (Woody Allen) in "Love & Death"

BILL KERN'S FAVORITE SPORTS LEGENDS

Spins the stories of great sports legends in "Radio Days" and the story of an armless, peg-legged pitching great "with heart".

BIRSKY, DR (Paul Nevens)

Neurologist who diagonses Zelig's condition as the result of a brain tumor and dies two weeks later himself of a brain tumor in "Zelig".

BLAIR, MISS (Jacquelyn Hyde)

Blackmails Virgil at work by threatening to expose his criminal past until he attacks her by driving his car into her apartment and blowing her up with dynamite in "Take the Money & Run"

BLUE MOONGLOW

Perfume worn by Ariel (Mia Farrow) in "Midsummer's Night Sex Comedy".

BLUM, JOHN MORTON

Author of Interprting Zelig in, what else, "Zelig".

BOB

A member of Lacey's entorauge in "Annie Hall".

BOGART, HUMPHREY (Jerry Lacy)

Counsels loser-in-love Alan Felix (Woody Allen) on how to meet with success with women in the play/film "Play It Again, Sam".

BOND, JIMMY (Woody Allen)

Deadly threat to the universe played by Allen in the Bond spoof, "Casino Royale" finally undone by his own exploding aspirin and a script that wasn't his own.

BOURNE, MEL

Production designer extraordinarre.

BOW, CLARA

Invites Zelig for the weekend and tells him to bring all his personalities.

BOWL OF STEAM

Gourmet meal served to the chain gang in "Take The Money & Run".

BRANDEIS UNIVERSITY

Well known liberal arts school with a predominantly Jewish enrollment in Waltham, MA which is a frequent target of Woody Allen's barbs second only to NYU, his alma matta..sort of. Still refuses to accept an honorary degree because it would require a trip through a tunnel. Cited in "Annie Hall" and "Hannah & Her Sisters".

IN MANHATTAN:
YALE: You are so self-righteous, you know. I
mean we're just people, we're just human
beings. You think you're god.
IKE: I gotta model myself after someone.

BREAKFAST W/ IRENE AND ROGER

Popular radio show in "Radio Days"

BRILL, NANCY (Cybill Shepherd)

Friend of Alice's who is now an important television executive who won't give her the time of day in "Alice".

BROADWAY BACHELORS

Film starring Gil Shepherd mentioned in "The Purple Rose Of Cairo"

BROADWAY DANCE PALACE

Club Tom Baxter takes Cecilia to when he brings her on-screen in "The Purple Rose Of Cairo".

BROCKMAN, DEBBIE

Sandy's sister whom he visits in "Starudst Memories".

BROCKMAN, SANDY

Sandy's original name before he changed it to Bates in "Stardust Memories".

BROWN, GARRETT

Actor who played Zelig in the Warner Bros. docu-pic "The Changing Man".

"Uh, uh, darling, sweetheart, darling may I, might I interject one nation at this juncture"
— Danny Rose (Woody Allen) to Tina Vitale in "Broadway Danny Rose"

CANOVA, LOU (Nick Apollo Forte)

Singer whose career Danny Rose tries to salvage in "Broadway Danny Rose"

CANOVA, TERESA

Lou's wife in "Broadway Danny Rose"

CARLYLE CLUB

Where Bobby Short plays in "Hannah and Her Sisters" during a date between Mickey Sachs (Woody Allen) and Holly (Dianne Weist) which Sachs says was about as "much fun as the Nurenberg Trials".

CARNEGIE DELI

Popular Manhattan eatery featured in "Broadway Danny Rose" where the comics assemble to tell their stories.

CAROL (Joanna Gleason)

Tony Roberts' wife in "Hannah" who is shocked when Mickey (Woody Allen) asks her husband to have a baby with his wife because he is impotent.

CASTELLI GALLERY

Exhibit where Yale and Mary run into Isaac and Tracy in "Manhattan"

FROM LOVE & DEATH:
SONIA: "Since this may be your
last night on earth let's go back to
my room and make love"
BORIS: "Nice idea, I'll bring the soy
sauce."

CECILIA (Mia Farrow)

The lovelost heroine of "The Purple Rose Of Cairo" who dreams of a better life by going to the movies.

CENTRAL PARALLEL OF AMERICAN FEDERATION

The area where Miles Monroe is discovered frozen in suspended animation in "Sleeper". Best known for its lack of area McDonalds.

"CHAMELEON DAYS"

Song sung by Mae Questel (Mother in "New York Stories") in "Zelig"

CHAPMAN, MICHAEL

Director of photography on "The Front"

CHARLES, MONICA (Diane Keaton)

Songstress who entertains the nightclub patrons in "Radio Days", a notable cameo for Keaton.

CHARLIE CHAPLIN

Former owner of Tony Lacey's house and popular old-time comedian.

CHIPPEWA FALLS

Annie Hall's hometown.

IN ZELIG:
Q: "What's brown and white and
yellow and has four eyes"
A: "Leonard Zelig at the League of
Nations"

CHOMSKY, PHIL

Manager of Weinstein's Majestic Bungalow Colony in the Catskills who books acts from Danny Rose in "Broadway Danny Rose".

CHRISTIE, DICK (Tony Roberts)

Close friend of Alan Felix's in "Play It Again, Sam" who is constantly dolling out his new phone number to his service.

CHRISTIE, LINDA (Diane Keaton)

Neuotic wife of Dick's who has an adulterous affair with Alan in "Play It Again, Sam"

CHRISTIE, TOM

NBC exeuctive, not related to Dick or Linda, who Alvy thinks is anti-Semetic when he clearly hears him say "did Jew eat?" Not did you eat? Clearly something for the Anti-Defamation League to look into.

CHRYSLER BUILDING

Art deco building from the twenties shown off during an impomptu tour of Manhattan in "Hannah & Her Sisters"

CLARK, EDDIE

Client of Danny Rose's whose penguin ice-skates dressed like a rabbi in "Broadway Danny Rose"

"Well, you know my Uncle Morris, the famous diabetic from Brooklyn used to say, `If you hate yourself, then you hate your work.'
— Danny Rose in "Broadway Danny Rose"

CLOQUET, GHISLAIN

Director of photography on "Love and Death"

CLUB HARLEM

Club Tom takes Cecilia to when they step into the film "The Purople Rose Of Cairo"

COBRA

Bartender in "What's Up Tiger Lily" who plans to marry his snake to a chicken

COLONEL DIAZ (Rene Enriquez)

Attends dinner with the President of San Marcos and Fielding Mellish in "Bananas".

COSELL, HOWARD

Famous "Wide World Of Sports" commentator featured in both "Bananas" and "Broadway Danny Rose". Also featured in "Sleeper" when the future society speculates that Cosell was used to torture prisoners in the mid-70's.

COSMETIC SEXUAL TECHNIQUES & POETRY

Class Luna took at the University in "Sleeper". Must have been a liberal arts school.

FROM STARDUST MEMORIES:
DAISY: What do you do, for
example, for laughs?
SANDY: ...Get undressed and
perform the Heimlich maneuver
on a loved one

COSTIKYAN, ANDREW

Director of photography of "Bananas"

COUNTESS ALEXANDROVNA (Olga Georges-Picot)

One of most enticing women in St. Petersburg (or in a Woody Allen movie) who seduces Boris (Woody Allen) in "Love & Death". Reputed for her insatiable sexual appetites.

COUSIN SONIA (Diane Keaton)

Boris (Woody Allen) cousin with whom he is in love but who loves his brother, Ivan in "Love & Death".

CRAIG, SHARON

Miss America testifies against Fielding Mellish in "Bananas"

CRAIG, WINDY

Universal Newsreel announcer in "Zelig"

CRAZY HORSE SALOON

Where all the nubile dancers work in "What's New Pussycat" and where Victor (Woody Allen) is employed...he pays them.

CRIST, JUDITH

The noted film critic played a cabaret show patron in "Starudst Memories"

"In your world things have a way of working out right. See, I'm a real person. No matter how...how tempted I am, I have to choose the real world."
— Cecilia (Mia Farrow) to Tom Baxter (Jeff Daniels) in "The Purple Rose Of Cairo"

CUMMINGS, E.E.

Ever since "Hannah & Her Sisters", he has provided the standard seduction line of young college freshman. On page 112, Elliot (Michael Caine) asks Lee to look at the poem in hopes of arousing her desire for him.

D'ANGELO, BEVERLY

Star of the VACATION movies who has a cameo as an actor in Rob's TV show in "Annie Hall".

DAD HALL (Donald Symington)

Annie's father.

DAISY

The sheep that Stavros Milos brings to Gene Wilder in "Everything You Wanted to Know About Sex" whom the doctor falls in love with.

DAISY (Jessica Harper)

Troubled and brooding woman who attends the Bates' film festival in "Stardust Memories" and goes to see "The Bicycle Thief" with Sandy.

DALTON SCHOOL

Where Tracy (Mariel Hemingway) goes to school in Manhattan and probably where Satchel will go.

*"Well, you've heard it with your own eyes"
— Howard Cosell in "Bananas" telecasting from a live political assassination*

DAVIS, ISAAC (Woody Allen)

TV comedy writer played by Woody Allen in "Manhattan" who abandons the boob tube in hopes of writing the great Americna novel.

DAVIS, JILL (Meryl Streep)

Davis' bisexual ex-wife who is writing a book about their relationship in "Manhattan".

DEATH AND WESTERN THOUGHT

Book Alvy gives to Annie as a present in "Annie Hall" in hopes of broadening her horizons.

DECHESER, ARTIE

Hannah's twins in "Hannah & Her Sisters"

DEGHEUEE, PAUL (John Rothman)

Eudora Fletcher's first cousin, inventor and photographer, who shoots the white room sessions in "Zelig".

DELILAH

Maid to Miss Ruth in "Purple Rose Of Cairo".

DEMPSEY, JACK

Meets Zelig, spars with him jokingly in "Zelig".

"God, she's beautiful"
— Michael Caine on Lee as she walks into
the room in "Hannah & Her Sisters"

DIANE (Elaine Stritch)

Troubled matriach of the clan in the antitdote to insominia, "September" originally played by Maureen O'Sullivan in Woody's first take on the film which was discarded for this reshoot. No relation to Diane Eisenberg who co-wrote this section of the book

DIMITRI

Boris' father who wants to build on a small piece of land he holds in his hand.

DINE & DANCE

Restaruant where Tom discovers he has no money in "The Purple Rose Of Cairo" while taking Cecilia on a date.

DIPALMA, CARLO

Director of photography on "Hannah" and "September"

DONNY

Mary's troubled analyst in "Manhattan" who has a bad acid experience.

DORRIE (Charlotte Rampling)

The psychologically unbalanced ex-lover of Sandy Bates' in "Stardust Memories"

"It's my life, I gotta do what's right for it."
— Lou Canova speaks the words every talent agent fears in "Broadway Danny Rose"

DOUG

College professor Lee sees and, finally, marries in the wake of her affair with Elliot in "Hannah & Her Sisters"

DOWD, THOMAS

Chief of Police who leads the "Zelig" manhunt.

DR. BERNARDO (John Carradine)

Scientest who was the first to explain the connection between excessive masturbation and entering politics in "Everything You Wanted To Know About Sex But Were Afraid To Ask"

DR. CHOMSKY

Isaac's analyst in "Manhattan"

DR. YANG (Keye Luke)

Prescribes the magic herbs which help Alice Tait turn invisible, see her dead ex-boyfriend and turn her life around in Alice.

DUANE HALL (Christopher Walken)

Have you sometimes felt like steering your car into oncoming traffic. Duane has. Brother of Annie.

"What do you want me to say? I don't want to make funny movies anymore. They can't force me to. I don't feel funny. I look around the world, and all I see is human suffering."
— Sandy Bates (Woody Allen) in "Starddust Memories"

DUCK SOUP

The film that saved Mickey's life in "Hannah". Seeing this Marx Brothers classic restored his will to live and enjoy life.

DUNN, BARNEY

The world's worst ventriloquist, Danny Rose says he "bearded" for Barney to his captors believing that Barney was out of the country only to find out he had cancelled his plans.

EDDIE (Alec Baldwin)

Ghost of ex-lover of Alice in "Alice". "Bottoms, no tops—could've told you," he says of Alice's yuppie husband Doug.

EL VERDE

The sandwich shop from which Fielding gets lunch for his hungry rebel troops.

EL WEIRDO

The original title for the film "Bananas".

EMILY (Anne Byrne)

The lover of Meryl Streep in "Manhattan".

*"Human beings are divided into mind
and body. The wind embraces all the
nobler aspirations like poetry and
philosophy. But the body has all the
fun...and God is an underachiever."
— Boris (Woody Allen) in "Love & Death"*

EPSTEIN

Runs into the courtroom confessing in the case of Epstein Vs. Epstein realizing he's in the wrong courtroom in "Bananas"

EPSTEIN, JULIUS

Prison psychiatrist who discusses Louise's influence on Virgil in "Take The Money And Run"

ESPOSITO (Jacobo Morales)

Rebel leader turned crazed dicator in "Bananas". Among his mandates are that the national language be changed to Swedish, all citizens must change their underwear every half hour and wear it on the outside and all children not 16 are now 16.

EXECU-TIZER

Device to help busy executives get their exercise without ever pausing in their daily schedule in "Bananas" product tested by Fielding Melish.

EXISTENTIAL MOTIFS IN RUSSIAN LITERATURE

Course Annie takes at Columbia where she meets David, her professor. The motto, of course, in Woody Allen movies is college is a good place for women to pick up eligible young college professors.

"It's very hard to get your heart and head together in life. In my case they're not even friendly"
— Cliff in "Crimes and Misdemeanors"

FABRIZIO (Woody Allen)

Italian producer who can't arouse his frigid wife in "Everything You Wanted To Know About Sex"

FACE TO FACE

Film playing at the Beekman Theatre in "Annie Hall" directed by Ingmar Bergman that Annie and Alvy miss the first two minutes of resulting in Alvy forcing them to go and see "The Sorrow And The Pity".

FAHTER DONNELLY (Milo O'Shea)

Confused man of the cloth starring in the film within a film "The Purple Rose Of Cairo".

FARROW, MOSES

One of Mia's children who has a featured role in "Hannah"

FASSBENDER, FRITZ (Peter Sellers)

The psychistrist who can't seem to meet women who counsels Peter O'Toole who can't stop seem meeting women in "What's New Pussycat?"

FAT, WING (Susumu Kurobe)

The evil, unscrupulous villain in "What's Up Tiger Lily?" desperately searching for the secret egg salad recipie.

"What does this man have to suffer about? Doesn't the man know he's got the greatest gift that anyone could have. The gift of laughter."
— Studio Executive Taylor in "Stardust Memories"

FATHER ANDRE (Leib Lensky)

Mickey Sachs consults him about Catholicism in "Hannah & Her Sisters"

FATHER NIKOLIA (C.A.R. Smith)

Tells a young Boris (Woody Allen) that all Jews have horns and stripes in "Love & Death". That's Russia for you.

FATOSH, PRINCESS

After she receives a snakebite on her breast, Fielding, along with all the rest of the men in the rebel camp, try to volunteer to suck out the poison in "Bananas"

FELDMAN, CHARLES K.

Producer of "What's Up Pussycat" and "Casino Royale".

FELIX, ALAN (Woody Allen)

29 year old aspirin junkie and star of "Play It Again Sam" who's just been dumped by his wife, Nancy.

FELIX, NANCY (Susan Anspach)

Alan Felix's wife, who after seeing `Easy Rider' dumps Alan (Allen) in hopes of a more exciting life.

"I can only hope that she was mine. With you as her mother, her father could have been anybody in Actors Equity"
—Evan to Norma in "Hannah & Her Sisters"

FERD, DULCY (Julie Hagerty)

One of the women who spends time frolicing in "A Midsummer Nights Sex Comedy". Scored with more laughs in "Airplane".

FESEY, DR.

Doesn't agree with Eudora Fletcher about Zelig's malady and suggests experimental drugs as the answer to Zelig's problem.

FINKLESTEIN, SYDNEY

Character Sandy plays in one of his films being shown at film festival whose hostility has escaped to ravage the countryside.

FISHER, CARRIE

Princess Leia plays April in "Hannah & Her Sisters" and also stars in the Allen-esque "When Harry Met Sally"

FLETCHER, CAHTERINE

Eudora's mom who doesn't provide for a very good radio interview in "Zelig".

FLETCHER, EUDORA DR. (Mia Farrow/Ellen Garrison)

Tries to determine the cause of Zelig's problem in "Zelig" and looks for a cure. She ultimately marries the changing man.

"Naturally I get taken home first. Well, obviously he prefers April. Of course I was so tongue tied all night. I can't believe I said that about the Guggenheim. My stupid little roller skating joke. I should never tell jokes."
— Holly in "Hannah & Her Sisters"

FLETCHER, MERYL

Sister to Eudora, who lives in Teaneck and an accomplished pilot.

FLICKER, DOCTOR

Alvy's mother has him talk to him in "Annie Hall" when he explains he isn't doing his homework because the universe is expanding. "It won't be expanding for billions of years yet, Alvy. And we gotta try to enjoy ourselves while we're here."

FOSTER, T.S.

Department of Corrections, Union City, NJ who is Virgil's first probation officer in "Take The Money And Run"

FOX, LITA (Deborah Rush)

Showgirl who claims she's married to Zelig from a previous incarnation and ignites a scandal in "Zelig".

FRANCISCO, DON (Lloyd Battista)

Woody impersonates him as part of a plot to assassinate Napoleon in "Love & Death".

FRANK'S RESTUARANT

Sandy brings Isobel and kids there for ice-cream.

"What if there is no God, what if we're a bunch of absurd people running around with no rhyme or reason"
— Boris ponders in "Love & Death"

FRANKLIN, JOE

Has Lou Canova on his show in "Broadway Danny Rose".

FREDDY K

Fishing boat that takes Danny across the Hudson River in "Broadway Danny Rose"

FRICKS

An ex-con who plays the role of director in Virgils' bankrobbing scene in which he and his cohorts pretend to be shooting a movie in "Take The Money & Run".

FRYE, DUSTY (Daniel Stern)

Wealthy rock star looking to buy some wall art from Frederick (Max Van Sydow) in "Hannah & Her Sisters". "I don't sell my art by the yard," Frederick admonishes him.

FULMAN & WEISS

Nancy's law firm in "Play It Again, Sam"

GAIL (Julie Kavner)

Mickey Sach's assistant on his television show in "Hannah & Her Sisters"

*"I can't suck anybody's leg that
I'm not engaged to"
— Fielding Mellish (Woody Allen) in
"Bananas"*

SMYTHE, ED

Official from Standards & Practices who attempts to cancel the Ronald Reagan satire in "Hannah & Her Sisters".

NORMAN (Tony Roberts)

Successful TV producer and former partner of Mickey's in "Hannah & Her Sisters" now living on the West Coast.

GAMMAGE, PHIL

Invited by Hannah to Thanksgiving dinner for Holly (Dianne Weist) to meet and headmaster at her daughter's school. Holly: "He reminds me of Ichabod Crane. His Adam's papple keep s jumping up and down whenever he gets excited"

GEIBELL, MIKE

Writer for NY Daily Mirror who provides insight into "Zelig"

GEIST, MARTIN

Lover of Ruth Zelig who turns Leonard Zelig into a side-show attraction. When he discovers Ruth involved with a cowardly bullfighter, he shoots them both and himself as well.

GENERAL EQUIPMENT

Company Fielding Mellish worked for while employed as a product tester in "Bananas"

"Oh perfect, there's a guy with a pistol running after us and we're stuck in the middle of the Macy's Day Parade."
— Danny Rose chased in New Jersey the night before Thanksgiving in "Broadway Danny Rose"

GEORGE, THE CHAUFFER (David Lipman)

Arrested for mail fraud in "Stardust Memories"

GINA (Louise Lasser)

Fabrizio's (Woody Allen) frigid wife in "Everything You Always Wanted to Know About Sex..." who can only be sexually aroused in public places.

GINSBERG & COHEN

The robot tailors in "Sleeper" who speak in heavily accented Yiddish dialect utilized as part of Miles reorientation.

GLOVER, JOHN

Plays Actor/Boyfrined of Annie's in "Annie Hall".

GRAMMY HALL (Helen Ludlam)

Anti-Semitic grandmother of Annie Hall's who pictures Alvy as a rabbi while he's eating dinner with the family in "Annie Hall".

GRAND CENTRAL

The television show Howard (Woody Allen) fronted scripts for in "The Front" for blacklisted writers.

"What makes New York such a funny place is that there's so much tension and pain and misery here"
— Lester (Alan Alda) in "Crimes & Misdemeanors"

GREE, JOE

Inusrance man Virgil gets locked up with as a punishment for complaining while working on the chain gang in "Take The Money & Run".

GREENHUNT, ROBERT

Long-time Allen producer whose skill as a top New York based producer has been utilized by other filmmakers including Mike Nichols.

GREY, HELEN

Salesgirl from Wisconsin, another of Zelig's many wives.

GRILLED CHEESE SANDWICHES

Fielding Mellish (Woody Allen) orders nine hundred to satiate the starving rebel troops in "Bananas".

GRIMSBY, ROGER

Plays himself as a New York area newscaster in "Bananas"

GUNTY, MORTY

Old-time hysterical Jewish comedian who shares lunch with the comedians at the Carnegie in "Broadway Danny Rose". Father of Casting Director Lori Gunty.

"I need a valium the size of a hockey puck"
— Danny Rose tells Tina Vitale (Mia Farrow) in "Broadway Danny Rose"

HACK, SHELLY

Pre Charlies' Angels Hack plays "shallow and empty" street stranger in "Annie Hall" who Alvy asks for advice about a fulfilling sex life.

HALL, ANNIE (Diane Keaton)

Girlfriend of Alvy's who abandons him for the "Coast" in "Annie Hall"

HAMLISCH, MARVIN

Scored "Take The Money And Run" and "Bananas".

HANCOCK GRAMMAR SCHOOL

Where Virgil went to school before turning to a life of crime in "Take The Money And Run"

HAYDEN PLANETERIUM

A soaked Isaac Davis and Mary Wilke take refuge during a rainstorm in the Planeterium where Isaac contemplates "committing interstellar perversity on the lunar surface".

HEADLEY, GLENNE

Popular actress and star of "Dirty Rotten Scoundrels" and "Dick Tracy" plays a hooker in "The Purple Rose of Cairo".

HEMPLE, STUART

The cartoonist who illustrated the long-running syndicated comic strip IN-SIDE WOODY ALLEN

HENRY (Edward Herrmann)

A member of the on-screen "Purple Rose Of Cairo" company.

HERBIE

Has a coming home party in 1945 at Alvy's house under the rollercoaster in Coney Island.

HERLIHY, ED

Announced for Pathe Newsreels in "Zelig"

HILDA (June Squibb)

Black housekeeper to Alice Tait in "Alice".

HIP BAGEL

Where Alan met his wife Nancy waiting tables in "Play It Again Sam"

HOLLANDER, MARIAN (Estelle Parsons)

Star of feature film based on Woody ALlen play "Don't Drink The Water"

"Oh, please, I have to go. I have to get my teeth cleaned"
— Lee to Elliot in "Hannah & Her Sisters"

HOLLANDER, WALTER (Jackie Gleason)

Star of feature film based on Woody Allen play "Don't Drink The Water"

HONEYMOON IN HAITI

Film of Gil Shepherd's in "Purple Rose Of Cairo"

HOOVER, EDGAR J. (Dorthi Fox)

Takes the stand against Fielding Mellish in "Bananas" disguised as a radical black woman.

HORGAN, PATRICK

Narrator on "Zelig"

HOT BOY

Club Tom takes Cecilia to after CopaCabana in "Purple Rose Of Cairo"

HOUSEMAN, DR.

Attributes Zelig's tendency as "glandular in nature", problem in secretions.

HOWARD (Denholm Elliot)

The next door neighbor of the inordinately boring family in "September"

"I don't travel by water, it's a against my religion"
— Danny Rose on approaching
the Freddie K in "Broadway Danny
Rose"

HUMMERS, WILLIAM

Recruited by Virgil to rob a bank; wanted for —among other crimes — getting naked in front of his in-laws in "Take The Money & Run".

HUNT, RANDOLPH

Drunk again at boat basin in Chippewa falls, says Dad Hall in "Annie Hall"

HYMAN, DICK

Music Composer and adapter for Woody whose films feature sparse original accompaniment, but are rather tracked by Woody with classic big band music from the '40s.

IGOR (Ray Sanchez)

The result of a botched experiment in which Dr. Bernardo gave him a four hour orgasm in "Everything You Wanted To Know About Sex"

IRENE

Raped and beaten, friend of Debbie's; Sandy Bates' sister in "Stardust Memories".

ISOBEL (Marie-Christie Barrault)

French girlfriend of Sandy's who returns to France after Sandy calls out ex-lover "Dorrie's" name in "Stardust Memories"

*"What's the universe got to do
with it? You're here in Brooklyn!
Brooklyn is not expanding!"
— Mother to Alvy in "Annie Hall"*

IT HAD TO BE YOU

Nightclub Annie sings at in her first appearance.

IVAN (Henry Czarniak)

Boris' brother stabbed to death by a Polish conscientious objector and object of Sonia's affections in "Love & Death".

IVONAVICH, ANTON (Harold Gould)

Famous for his temper challenges Boris to a duel to the death when he learns of Boris' midnight tryst with his lover.

JAFFE, BERNARD

First guest on "What's My Perversion" who enjoys exposing himself on subways in "Everything You Wanted To Know About Sex..".

JAMES, MICHAEL (Peter O'Toole)

Irrestisible womanizer in "What's Up Pussycat"

JAYSON, HERBIE

Bird trick client of Danny Rose's whose bird PeeWee is eaten by a cat in "Broadway Danny Rose".

ON BASKETBALL:
"What is so fascinating about a group of pituitary cases trying to stuff the ball through a hoop"
— Robin, Alvy's second wife, to Alvy in "Annie Hall"

JEREMIAH (Wallace Shawn)

Mary's ex-husband, the man "who totally opened me up sexually", she says played by the overweight, balding playwright best known as the star of "My Dinner With Andre" and "The Princess Bride".

JEWEL THEATRE

The theatre exhibiting "The Purple Rose Of Cairo" managed by Irving Metzman.

JOFFE, CHARLES

Longtime Allen manager and producer with Jack Rollins who first represented Allen as a stand-up.

JULIE (Joy Bang)

A girl who works in Dick Christie's office who just broke up a romance and dates Alan Felix in "Play It Again, Sam" but is abandoned by him when a band of biker's approach her.

JENNIFER (Viva)

Second blind date set up by the Christies played by Warhol girl Viva who also rebuffs the sex-starved Felix.

KAGI NO KAGI

The original Japanese title of the film which was adapted into "What's Up Tiger Lily?"

"I especially like your early funny ones"
— Mrs. Payson tells Bates in "Stardust Memories"

KAISER WILHELM

After being hit on the head at a baseball game, Virgil's grandfather thinks he is Kaiser Wilhelm, the ruler of Germany during World War I in "Take the Money And Run".

KAWALSKY

The man the warden's daughter was kissing when Virgil attempts to use her as a hostage during his prison break in "Take The Money & Run" after his gun, made of soap, lathers into nothingness in the rain.

KEATON, MICHAEL

Originally supposed to play Tom Baxter/Gil Shephed deemed too contemporary by Allen after a week of shooting and replaced by Jeff Daniels.

KLEINER

Film exexutive in "Stardust Memories" who considers Bates' work indulgent.

KNOX, APRIL (Carrie Fisher)

Founder of the Stanislavski Catering Company with Holly and an aspiring actress.

KOSLOW, CHARLES (Richard Litt)

Eudora Fletcher's attorney lover in Zelig who she abandons to marry Leonard.

ON NOVELIZATIONS:
"It's like another contemporary
American phenomenon that's
truly moronic, the novelizations of
movies."
— Isaac to Mary in "Manhattan"

KRIM, STANLEY

Aviation photographer who filmed Virgil being captured by FBI.

KUEHN, JURGEN

German U.F.A. Newsreel photographer.

LACEY, TONY (Paul Simon)

Satire on Warren Beatty, music producer who convinces Annie to come West to cut an album in "Annie Hall".

LAKE, SHARON (Jennifer Salt)

Tells Alan Felix she starred in the film "Gang Bang" and another of his unfortuante blind dates in "Play It Again, Sam".

LANDIS, MR.

Official interpreter when Fielding comes to the United States under the guise of a visiting dignitary in "Bananas"

LANE (Mia Farrow)

The troubled daughter of "September" who shot her mother's second husband, a gangster.

LASSER, LOUISE

Allen's second wife and star of many of his early films.

*"I had a great time tonight, really.
It was like the Nuremberg Trials."
— Woody to Holly on a really bad
date in "Hannah & Her Sisters"*

LENARD, MARK

Sarek from Star Trek played a Navy officer during a brief scene in "Annie Hall"

LEONARD THE LIZARD

Leonard Zelig's monicker and subject of a popular dance craze.

LESTOR (Alan Alda)

Narcissitic television producer in "Crimes & Misdemeanors" played by M*A*S*H's Alda, a narcissitic television producer/actor/writer/director.

LEVINE, R.H.

The writer of the fictitious "Purple Rose Of Cairo"

LEVY, LOUIS (Martin Bergmann)

Speaker on God and Love who Cliff is putting together a documentary about who commits suicide in "Crimes & Misdemeanors"

LEWIS, KAY (Louise Lasser)

Woman interviewed about Virgil in "Take The Money & Run". "I actually believed that he was idiot...now I think he's brilliant."

LIBERTY VIEW DINER

Where Tina and Danny Rose stop to eat on their way to Lou's show at the Waldorf in Manhattan.

LISA (Mia Farrow)

Sheldon's "shiksa" girlfriend in "Oedipus Wrecks" who leaves him when his mother starts denegrating her from her perch in the sky above Manhattan.

LLOYD (Jack Warden)

Replaced Charles Durning as the physicist now married to Diane (Elaine Stritch) in "September"

LOUISE (Janet Margolin)

Virgil attempts to rob her purse in "Take The Money And Run" but falls in love with her instead and tells her he's with the New York Philharmonic.

LOVIN' SPOONFUL

Perform theme song in "What's Up Tiger Lily" and appear in several cameo appearances edited into the Japanese film.

LOWRY, DOROTHY

School teacher who remembered Virgil stealing her fountain pen initiating his life of crime in "Take The Money And Run".

"Rebels are We! Born to be Free!
Just like the fish in the sea"
— Rebel fight anthem from
"Bananas" and "Sleeper"

LUCY JONES MODELING AGENCY

Modelling agency that supplied model hired on "What's My Perversion".

LYND, VESPER (Ursula Andress)

The sultry collaborator who works with Peter Sellers in "Casino Royale" pretending to be James Bond.

MAHARISHI (Ved Bardbu)

Appears at Madison Square Garden where Alvy is on a date with a reporter for Rolling Stone played by Shelly Duvall.

MALIGNANT MELANOMA

What Mickey Sachs thought he had before believing he had a brain tumor in "Hannah & Her Sisters"

MANHATTAN HOSPITAL

Where Zelig was admitted when his condition was discovered.

MANON LESCAUT

Performed in the opera David and Holly went to see in "Hannah & Her Sisters"

"I hate to tell you this is 1975, you know that `neat' went out, I would say, at the turn of the century."
— Alvy to Annie on her choice of adjectives in "Annie Hall"

MARRIAGE, DIVORCE AND SELFHOOD

Book Jill (Meryl Streep) writes about her ill-fated relationship with Issac in "Manhattan" and how he tried to run her lover over with a car.

MARTINEZ, LUIS

Cowardly bullfighter Ruth Zelig meets and falls in love with who is killed by Martin Geist in "Zelig"

MASKED AVENGER SECRET COMPARTMENT RING

For only 15 cents this can be yours. Results in a Young Woody appropriating money for the establishment of the State Of Israel to buy a ring in "Radio Days".

MASON, PAMELA

Plays herself on 'What's My Perversion?' in "Everything/Sex".

MAVIS

One of Woody's black maids in "Hannah & Her Sisters".

MAX

Rob's (Tony Roberts) name for Alvy in "Annie Hall" which is also the pseudonym Allen uses in public so people won't realize its him.

"Where did April come up with that stuff about Adolph Loos and terms like `organic form'? Well naturally, she went to Brandeis."
— Holly in "Hannah & Her Sisters"

MAXIMOVITCH, VLADIMIR (Tony Jay)

A member of Boris' brigade going into action against the French.

MAXWELL, LEN

Renown voiceover talent and Catskill comedian who plays interviewer in "What's Up Tiger, Lily" and collaborated with Allen on the film. Also known as the voice of Punchy, the Kool-Aid mascot.

MAYERSON, HENRY DR.

Part of team from Manhattan Hospital assigned to determine if Zelig is cured.

McLUHAN , MARSHAL

Television scholar and critic who Alvy introduces to a blustering Columbia Professor in "Annie Hall" to disproves his inane hypothesis.

MELAMED, FRED

Well known voiceover talent who plays Dr. Grey in "Hannah & Her Sisters"

MELINKOFF, DOCTOR

Tells Sandy to stop using shampoo solution in "Stardust Memories" because it has been determined to cause cancer.

"Sex alleviates tension, love causes it"
— Andrew in "Midsummer Nights Sex Comedy"

MELLISH, FIELDING (Woody Allen)

Nebbishy product tester who goes to San Marcos to reconcile a waning relationship in "Bananas" and becomes El Presidente.

MELLISH, RUTH (Charlotte Rae)

Fielding's mother in "Bananas".

MENDELSSOHN

Composer whose music provided the score to "A Midsummer Nights Sex Comedy"

MERSON'S PEST CONTROL

Teddy Ashcroft's exterminator company, mice and silverfish a speciality, in "Purple Rose Of Cairo".

METRO

Where Mickey goes to see Marx Bros. "Duck Soup" in "Hannah &Her Sisters"

MICHAEL'S PUB

Popular and overpriced Manhattan bistro where Woody plays clarinet every Monday evening with his "New Orleans Ragtime Funeral Band"

*"I have to go now, Duane,
because I'm due back on Planet
Earth"
— Alvy to Duane Hall (Christopher
Walken) in "Annie Hall"*

MILLER, DANIEL

FBI agent and author of the book "Mother Was A Red"

MILLS, SHELDON (Woody Allen)

Lawyer in "Oedipus Wrecks" segment of NEW YORK STORIES whose nagging mother disappears during a magic show only to reappear in the skies above Manhattan.

MILLSTEIN, SHELDON

Sheldon's original name before he changed it to Mills.

MILOS, STAVROS (Titos Vandis)

Armenian shepherd who brings sheep, Daisy, to Gene Wilder in hopes of reconciling a love relationship with it because he believes the sheep no longer loves him in "Everything You Wanted To Know About Sex But Were Afraid To Ask".

MINSK

Site of village idiots convention in "Love & Death"

MISS TERIAKI & HER SISTER SUKI

Phil's two asistants recruited to find the secret egg salad recipie in "What's Up Tiger Lily?"

"Where I grew up in Brooklyn no one committed suicide - everyone was so unhappy"
— Cliff in "Crimes & Misdemeanors"

MOM HALL (Colleen Dewhurst)

Annie's mother in "Annie Hall"

MONK (Danny Aiello)

Cecilia's abusive husband in "Purple Rose Of Cairo"

MORSE, SUSAN

Longtime film editor of Allen's films.

MOSKOWITZ, PHIL (Tatsuya Mihashi)

Lovable rogue hero of "What's Up Tiger Lily". "Take that you bohemian fruitcake vegetable fornicator..." Searches for the secret egg salad recipie.

MOSKOWITZ, SID (Bob Balaban)

Second man to confess to Alice that he loves her after drinking spiked egg nog with Dr. Yang's magic herbs.

MOSKOWITZ, TESSIE (Rachel Novikoff)

They say she was a great beauty with personality; Alvy's aunt in "Annie Hall".

MOTHER STARKWELL (Ethel Sokolow)

Virgil's mother who dons a disguise during the mock documentary "Take The Money & Run"

"Some Jews are smart although I hear their wives don't believe in sex after marriage"
— Boris to his regiment in "Love & Death"

MOTT HOTEL

Where Virgil rents a cheap room after being paroled from prison

MOUNT SINAI HOSTPITAL

Where Mickey Sachs receives his tests fearing the worst in "Hannah & Her Sisters"

MR. BARNES (Ira Wheeler)

The law partner who has a mistress, says Sheldon's mother played by Mae Questel in "New York Stories".

MR. RUSKIN

Ticket taker at the Jewel theatre in "The Purple Rose Of Cairo"

MUNK, JONATHAN

Brother of Robert who played a young Woody Allen in "Love and Death".

MUNK, JONATHAN

P:lays Alvy Singer at age 9 in "Annie Hall"

MUNK, ROBERT

Played Sandy as young boy in "Radio Days".

"I never saw so many reeds in my life. I feel like Moses"
— Danny Rose after eluding the hit men in the swamp in "Broadway Danny Rose"

MUSEUM OF MODERN ART

Where Isaac runs into Mary during a benefit for the ERA sponsored by Bella Abzug in "Manhattan"

JERRY

Friend of Isaac's at MOMA benefit

NANCY (Louise Lasser)

the woman at Fielding's door with petition requesting that US break ties with San Marcos saying that the U.S. should give full support to rebels, not dictators leading him to initiate a relationship.

NAPOLEON (James Tolkan)

The object of an assassination attempt by Sonia and Boris in "Love & Death" although they only kill an impersonator.

NATASHA (Jessica Harper)

Sonia's cousin whom she advises about love...and death in "Love & Death" after Boris is executed for attempting to kill Napoleon.

NICHOLI, UNCLE

One of Boris' uncles in "Love & Death"

"Some men are heterosexual and some men are bisexual. Some men don't think about sex at all and they become lawyers"
— Boris (Woody Allen) in "Love and Death"

NICHOLS, JOEY (Hy Ansel)

Annoying friend of Alvy's father who pulls nickels out of a young Alvy's ear in "Annie Hall". "What an asshole", he says.

NINA

Friend whom Alice (Mia Farrow) confides to about the man she is thinking about seeing while dropping her children at school in "Alice"

NOAH, DOCTOR (Woody Allen)

The nom de plum of Jimmy Bond who threatens the world with anhilation in "Casino Royale".

OG

Space creatures who come down and tell Sandy Bates to make funnier films and stop worrying about the human condition in "Stardust Memories".

OLD GREGOR

The younger brother of the Gregors in "Love & Death"

OLDA HAMPKIN (Georges Adet)

Serf who dies putting lightning rod up and is Boris' first exposure to death in "Love & Death"

"I still think you should turn the projector off and shut down. This could be the work of Reds, or anarchists"
— A newspaper reporter to theater manager Irving Metzman in "The Purple Rose of Cairo"

OLGA

Woman Cecilia (Mia Farrow) discovers with her husband, Joe Caruso's sister in "The Purple Rose Of Cairo".

ORGASM

Popular men's monthly Fielding tries to inconspiculously buy in "Bananas".

ORKIN, VIVIAN (Helen Hanft)

The moderator of the Sandy Bates' film culture weekend in "Stardust Memories"

PABST

Film executive who considers Bates' work indulgent in "Stardust Memories"

PAGE 112

Where e.e. cummings poem can be found.

PAGEANT BOOK & PRINT SHOP

Old bookstore in the village where Elliot buys Lee the e.e. Cummings book.

PALEY, DELORES (Angelica Huston)

Mistress of Judah Rosenthal (Martin Landau) whom he has killed when she threatens to expose their affair to his wife.

PAM (Shelly Duvall)

Rolling Stone reporter whom Alvy dates after breaking up with Annie in "Annie Hall".

PATROL MAN LYNCH

Discovers the chain gang passing themselves off as brothers in "Take The Money & Run"

PATROSNICH, GLADMIIR

Killed in the war with Napoleon, gives an engagement ring to Boris as Death takes him away.

PAYSONS

Charimen of the film culture weekend in "Stardust Memories"

PEARLMAN, DR.

Attended film festival, did paper on Bates at a psychiatric convention.

PEE WEE

Piano playing bird eaten by cat and number one act of Herbie Jayson who is represented by Danny Rose. Best known for his poignant rendering of "September Song."

*"Some men don't care about sex
at all, they become lawyers"
— Boris reflecting on his life in
"Love and Death"*

PENGUIN HOUSE

Central Park Zoo location where Alice suggests she rendezvous with Joe Ruffalo in "Alice".

PERLSTEIN, RABBI

Danny Rose's rabbi who tells Danny we are "all guilty in eyes of God"

PETER (Sam Waterston)

Rabbi who is going blind in "Crimes & Misdemeanors" and is attended and advised by opthomologist Judah Rosenthal.

PETERSON, OSCAR

"Blues For Alan Felix" jazz composition is featured in "Play It Again, Sam" and is where the Alan Felix's name is drawn from.

PETRONIA

A member of Tony Lacey's entourage

PHILBIN, REGIS

Plays himself in "What's My Perversion?" in "Everything You Wanted To Know About Sex"

"I turned Irish. My hair turned red, my nose turned up, spoke about the great potato famine and the little people."
— admits Zelig in a trance in "Zelig"

PIERRE HOTEL

Where Tony Lacey is staying in New York and meeting Jack Nicholson and Angelica Huston for drinks in "Annie Hall"

PINKUS PLUMBING COMPANY

The company a fellow student of Alvy's elementary school class is running today according to "Annie Hall"

PLATH, SYLVIA

Interesting poetess whose tragic suicide was misinterpreted as romantic by the college girl mentality, accoridng to Alvy

POHL, OSWALD

Former SS Obergruppenfuhrer who remarks about Eudora Fletcher's discovery of Zelig on the podium next to Hitler in "Zelig".

POLITICAL COMMITMENT IN TWENTIETH CENTURY LITERATURE

Allison Portchnik's thesis which she is working on while attending Brandeis in "Annie Hall".

POLLACK, EMILY

Yale's wife in "Manhattan"

WOODY ON ANNIE HALL:
"I wonder what she looks like naked?"
— Alvy thinks to himself in "Annie Hall"

POLLACK, YALE (Michael Murphy)

Friend of Isaac's in "Manhattan" who is having an affair with Mary Wilke. When they break-up he suggests Isaac date her only to leave his wife and re-unite with Mary.

PORTCHNIK, ALLISON (Carol Kane)

Alvy's second wife whom he meets at an Adlai Stevneson fundraiser in "Annie Hall"

PREVIN, DAISY

One of Mia's children featured in "Hannah & Her Sisters"

PROKOFIEV

Composer whose music provided the accompaniment for "Love & Death"

PUBLIC, JOHN Q.

False name Virgil gives while trying to get a job at insurance company in "Take The Money & Run"

PURPLE GROTTO

Popular Manhattan club Tom Baxter takes Cecilia to in "The Purple Rose Of Cairo".

"Sometimes to have a little good luck is the best plan of all"
— Sam Waterston to Judah (Martin Landau) in "Crimes & Misdemeanors"

RALPH

Guy who approaches Alvy at Beekman Theatre and wants his autograph made out to his wife.

RASH

Old man's wife who says he hated the film in "Stardust Memories" after the cast screening.

REED, HALLEY (Mia Farrow)

Associate producer of a popular news program whom Cliff grows infatuated with who marries Lester (Alan Alda) in "Crimes & Misdemanors".

REPTILE EYES

Sung by Rosemarie Jun in "Zelig".

REUBEN, DAVID DR.

Wrote the landmark book "Everything You Wanted To Know About Sex But Were Afraid To Ask" which the film was loosely based on.

RICH, ED

Representitive of NY Landmarks Comission who tries to recruit Bates for benefit in "Stardust Memories".

"I want you to enjoy me, my wry sense of humor and astonishing sexual technique, but never forget that, you know, you've got your whole life ahead of you."
— Isaac to Tracy in "Manhattan"

RISPOLI, JOE

One of Johnny's brothers sent to kill Danny Rose for stealing Tina away from him.

RISPOLI, JOHNNY

Lovestruck with Tina, he drinks a bottle of iodine to try and kill himself when he thinks Danny Rose has seduced her away from him.

RISPOLI, VITO

Johnny's other brother sent to kill Danny.

ROBIN (Janet Margolin)

Alvy's second wife in "Annie Hall", a psychiatrist who's prone to analyzing Alvy.

ROCCO

Tina's uncle, owns a fleet of cement mixers in "Broadway Danny Rose"

ROIGMAN, OWEN

Director of photography on "Play It Again, Sam"

ROLLINS, JACK

Played a studio executive in "Stardust", a comedian in "Danny Rose" and in real-life Woody's long time manager and executive producer.

WOODY ON ART & LIFE:
"You can't control life. It doesn't wind up
perfectly. Only art you can control. Art
and masturbation. Two areas in which I am
an absolute expert."
— Sandy Bates (Woody Allen) on life in
"Stardust Memories"

ROOSEVELT HOSPITAL

Where they take Barney Dunn after he is beat up by the Rispoli brothers who think Danny was bearding for him.

ROSE, MICKEY

High school friend of Allen's who collaborated on the scripts for "Take The Money And Run" and "Bananas".

ROSENBLUM, RALPH

Editorial consultant on Allen's earliest pictures and later full time editor until his assistant, Susan Morse took over.

ROSENTAHL, JUDAH (Martin Landau)

Opthamologist who grapples with morality and religion when he asks his brother to kill his mistress who threatens to expose their relationship to his wife. Resulted in Academy Award nomination for Landau.

ROSENTHAL, CLAIRE (Miriam Rosenthal)

Judah's wife in "Crimes & Misdemeanors"

ROSENTHAL, JACK (Jerry Orbach)

Judah's brother who offers to arrange for the killing of Delores in "Crimes and Misdemeanors".

"The last time I was inside a woman was when I visited the Statue of Liberty"
— Cliff on his sex life in "Crimes & Misdemeanors"

ROSS COUNTY

The county in which there is a small bank that Virgil plans to rob in "Take the Money & Run"

ROSS COUTNY CORRECTIONAL FARM

Where Virgil served as member of the chain gang in "Take The Money & Run" after another ill-fated bank robbery.

ROSS, DOCTOR (Gene Wilder)

After being repulsed by Stavros Milos request to talk to his sheep about why she doesn't love him anymore, gradually falls in love with the sheep and ends up taking the animal to bed in "Everything You Wanted To Know About Sex But Were Afraid To Ask"

ROSS, HERBERT

Directed "Play It Again, Sam" starring and written by Woody Allen.

RUFFALO, JOE (Joe Mantegna)

Single father and tenor saxaphone player attracted to Alice with whom she considers having an affair in "Alice".

RUFUS, HARRIET

"Douche bag" who says Monk" is pitching pennies and making passes at girls all day" in "The Purple Rose Of Cairo".

"Oh really. Somewhere Nabaokov is smiling, if you know what I mean."
— Mary says Yale about Isaac's 17 year old girlfriend Tracy in "Manhattan"

SACHS, MICKEY (Woody Allen)

Hannah's ex-husband, a troubled television writer who thinks he's dying in "Hannah & Her Sisters"

SAN MARCOS

The mythical banana republic that leads the world in social diseases.

SAN SIMEON

Hearst's xandadu where Zelig goes to enjoy himself after his triumphant return from abroad. Redubbed Xanadu in "Citizen Kane", Welles fictionilized version of Hearst's life.

SCHLOSSER, LUNA (Diane Keaton)

The renown poetess of the future with whom Miles falls in love and recruits to the rebel movement in "Sleeper"

"SEEMS LIKE OLD TIMES"

Annie sings this song at a club where she is discovered by record producer Tony Lacey in "Annie Hall".

SERETSKY, ALEXI, ALAGORIAN, ASAMOV

Some of Sonia's lovers in "Love & Death"

"The only absolute knowledge attainable by man is that life is meaningless"
— Tolstoy as quoted in "Hannah & Her Sisters"

SHAKAPOPOLIS, VICTOR (Woody Allen)

Allen's feature film persona in "Everything You Wanted To Know About Sex" and "What's New Pussycat"

SHANA (Gina Gallagher)

Joe's Rufalo's daughter in "Alice".

SHANDAR

Escape artist that Danny Rose used to handle before he left him for another agent.

SHANDAR THE MAGICIAN (George Schindler)

In "New York Stories" Shandar makes Sheldon's mother disappear...which Sheldon soon realizes isn't such a bad thing until she reappears in the sky above Manhattan.

SHANKAR, ALBERT

Former head of the New York Board of Education who, according to "Sleeper" is responsible for World War III, when he got ahold of a Nuclear bomb.

SHELLY

Female fan who wants to sleep with Sandy in "Stardust Memories"

SHEPHERD, GIL (Jeff Daniels)

Played Tom Baxter in "Purple Rose Of Cairo".

SHORR, LESTER

Director of photography for "Take The Money & Run"

SHORT, BOBBY

Played himself in "Hannah & Her Sisters"

SINDELL, ALLA, DR.

Issues statement from Manhattan Hospital about Zelig's condition.

SINGER, ALVY (Woody Allen)

The neurotic stand-up comedian who falls in love with Annie Hall.

SMITH, DR.

Tells Mickey and Hannah they can't have children in "Hannah & Her Sisters"

SMITH, GREGORY PAYNE WHITNEY

Guest on Issac's comedy show `Human Beings Wow!'

"The rest of the country looks upon New York like we're left wing, Communist, Jewish, homosexual, pornographers. I think of us that way sometimes — and I live here."
— Alvy to Rob in "Annie Hall"

SOMADRIL HYDRATE

Experimental drug used on Zelig

SORENSON, LISA

Trotskyite who became a Jesus freak and was arrested for selling pornographic connect the dots books in "Sleeper".

SPINER, BRENT

Star Trek actor who played a fan in the lobby in "Stardust Memories"

ST. REGIS HOTEL

Where Elliot and Lee have a secret tryst in "Hannah & Her Sisters"

ST. WAYNE

Prison where Virgil was incarcerated in "Take The Money & Run"

STALLONE, SYLVESTER

Street thug in "Bananas" who terrorizes Fielding on the subway.

STANHOPE CAFE

Mary and Yale call it quits on their affair, for the first time, in "Manhattan" in this four star hotel's elegant restaurant.

"I work mostly on the continent. I've written quite a few psychoanalytic papers. I studied a great deal, I worked with Freud in Vienna. We broke over the concept of penis envy. Freud felt that it should be limited to women."
— Leonard Zelig speaking as a psychiatrist

STANISLAVSKI CATERING COMPANY

Founded by Holly and April Knox, aspiring actresses to subsidize their cost of living.

STARDUST HOTEL

Where the film culture weekend to honor Sandy Bates is held

STARKELL, WILLIAM MRS.

Wife of NJ handyman gives birth to Virgil on December 1, 1935.

STARKWELL, VIRGIL (Woody Allen)

Criminal star of "Take The Money & Run"

STEPHANIE (Dianne Weist)

Troubled friend of Lane's in "September".

STERN, CLIFF (Woody Allen)

Documentary filmmaker who is hired by his brother-in-law, Lester to make a film about his career.

STERN, WENDY (Joanna Gleason)

Lester's sister, an English teacher who is divorcing Cliff.

"The saddest thing thing in the world is a missed opportunity" — Andrew says in "A Midsummer Night's Sex Comedy"

STONE, SHARON

Before she could totally recall Arnold in Verhoeven's film, she played a pretty girl on a train in "Stardust Memories"

STURGIS, LEOPOLD (Jose Ferrer)

The brooding intellectual of "Midsummer Nights Sex Comedy" who after dying during sex has his spirit inhabit the woods where their summer house is.

SULLIAN, MICHAEL

Ex-convict and one of the leaders of the planned prison break who forgets to tell Virgil the break is off and Virgil is caught during an attempt to escape when his gun fashioned out of soap lathers in the rain.

SUTTON, HENRY PORTER

Socialite and patron of the arts who invites F. Scott Fitzgerald to his party where he remarks about Zelig for the first time in print.

SWEDISH

The new national language of San Marcos.

SWERDLOW, STANLEY

Blames Zelig's condition on eating too much Mexican food.

"I'm a pacifist, I don't believe in war..I can't shower with other men"
— Boris on being drafted in "Love and Death"

TAIT, ALICE (Mia Farrow)

The troubled and unhappy housewife who uses Dr. Yang's herbs to escape her dreary life in "Alice".

TAIT, DOUG (William Hurt)

Alice's husband who is having myriad affairs and discourages Alice from pursuing her artistic yearnings.

TALMAGE, ROBERT

A member of the cast of "What's Up Tiger Lily?"

TANIGUCHI, SENKICHI

Director of the original Japanese version of "What's Up Tiger Lily?"

TATUM, MARIANNE

Actress who plays Eudora Fletcher in the Warner Bros. film "The Changing Man"

TAYLOR, JULIET

Allen's longtime casting director.

THE BICYCLE THIEF

Daisy and Sandy go to see the classic Vincent DeSica film in "Stardust Memories"

"As a boy, Leonard is frequently bullied by anti-Semites. His parents, who never take his part and blame him for everything side with the anti-Semites."
— Narrator Patrick Horgan in "Zelig"

THE CASTRATING ZIONIST

Short story Isaac is expanding into a novel in "Manhattan"

THE CHANGING MAN

1935 Warner Bros. movie about Zelig in "Zelig".

THE DENIAL OF DEATH

One of the books Alvy gives to Annie while they're dating.

THE EASTER PARADE

Elliot lends Lee this book in "Hannah & Her Sisters"

A DOLL'S HOUSE

Toast delivered by Evan, Hannah's father, complimenting her on her bravura performance in the play

THE GRAND EXHALTED HIGH MAKA OF PROSPER

"A non existent but real sounding country" on the waiting list for country-hood when some space opens on the map.

THE NEEDLEBAUMS

Upset to find their house has been robbed until a truck pulls up with all new furniture, the result of the robbers winning "Name That Tune" the night before in "Radio Days".

"I'm certain it's something he picked up from eating Mexican food"
— comments one doctor on Leonard Zelig's condition in "Zelig"

THE SORROW & THE PITY

"Four hour documentary about Nazis" Alvy and Annie go to see when they miss the beginning of FACE TO FACE.

THE WAY OF ZEN

Dorrie gives Sandy this book for his birthday in "Stardust Memories"

TINA

Isaac's first wife in "Manhattan" who went to EST and then became a Moonie and is now an agent at William Morris.

TOLCHIN, DAVID (Sam Waterston)

Architect who wines and dines Holly...and April in "Hannah & Her Sisters".

TONY (Tony Roberts)

The actor Roberts' plays in "Stardust Memories".

TORGMAN, A

Virgil's first and only cello teacher in "Take the Money And Run"

TOWER RECORDS

The best record store in New York where Mickey runs into Holly in the jazz section in "Hannah & Her Sisters"

"I'm a bigot, you know, but for the left"
— Alvy to Allison Porchnik (Carol Kane) in "Annie Hall"

TRACY (Mariel Hemingway)

Isaac's 17 year old girlfriend who is leaving for a scholarship to study acting in London in "Manhattan".

TREVA (Julie Kavner)

The phony mystic who tries to help Sheldon bring his mother down from the sky in "Oedipus Wrecks".

TURNER, CALVIN

Waiter at Chicago speakeasy who witnesses Zelig as a black drummer.

TURTURRO, JOHN

Plays a writer in "Hannah & Her Sisters".

TV MEDIA & CULTURE

Class at Columbia taught by annoying man in line in "Annie Hall" who finds "Fellini" indulgent and doesn't know anything about McLuhan.

UNION FIDELTY BANK

Bank Virgil and gang intend to rob in "Take The Money & Run"

VARGAS, EMILIO GENERAL (Carlos Montalban)

Overthrown dictator of San Marcos.

"I'm dating a girl wherein I can beat up her father. It's the first time that phenomenon ever occurred in my life."
— Isaac on his relationship with Tracy (Mariel Hemingway) in "Manhattan"

VITALE, TINA (Mia Farrow)

Mistress of Lou Canova's who ends up falling for Danny Rose.

VOLKAVICH, LEONID

Herring merchant who is weds Sonia (Diane Keaton) and is killed while cleaning his gun after her honor is challenged.

WAFFLES

Mary's Wilke's dog in "Manhattan", a dachushund.

"A penis substitute".

WALDORF ASTORIA

Where Lou Cannova appears on his comeback tour and is seen by Milton Berle and Howard Cosell.

WALTER, TRACY

Actor in Rob's TV show in "Annie Hall"

WASHINGTON SENATORS

It was at one of their games that Virgil's grandfather was hit by a ball and began thinking he was Kaiser Wilhelm.

"The thing to remember about comedy is if it bends it's funny, if it breaks it's not"
— Lester (Alan Alda) in "Crimes & Misdemeanors"

WATSON, SEYMOUR JUDGE (Arthur Hughes)

Presiding Judge in trial of the People Vs. Fielding Mellish.

WEAVER, SIGOURNEY

Pre-Alien Weaver is Alvy's fully-clad date in "Annie Hall". They run into Annie at "The Sorrow And The Pity".

WEBB, RAY

The actor in superhero costume shooting a commercial that Danny and Tina come upon while trying to escape the Rispoli brothers.

WEINSTEIN'S MAJESTIC BUNGALOW COLONY

Catskill Mountain's resort where many of Danny's best acts have been booked in "Broadway Danny Rose"

WEIST, DWIGHT

Hearst Metrotone news announcer in "Zelig".

WERNER, CAROL (Romy Schneider)

One of O'Toole's many female admirers in "What's New Pussycat"

WEYMOUTH, ARIEL (Mia Farrow)

The lovestruck woman of "A Midsummer's Night Sex Comedy".

"I've never seen such a sexy
classical violinist before. Usually,
they're escaped Hungarians."
— Alvy to Daisy (Jessica Harper) in
"Stardust Memories"

WHAT'S NEW PUSSYCAT

According to the Boston Phoenix, Allen described the experience this way: "I loathed everyone and everything concerned with it and they all loathe me. They butchered my script. They wrenched it into a commercial package...It ended up in the hands of establishment people who were hep, not hip, I couldn't go to see it for a year." Originally designed as a vehicle for Warren Beatty whose pick-up line was "What's New Pussycat?"

WHITNEY MUSEUM

Mary and Isaac go on a date at the Whitney after Yale breakups up with her.

WILDE, LARRY

Character the ensemble of "Purple Rose" is meeting at the Copocabana. They never do get there.

WILKE, MARY (Diane Keaton)

The problem plagued intellectual of "Manhattan" who is seeing Isaac's best friend, Yale.

WILKES, DR.

Mickey calls him to find out what a hearing loss might mean after his appointment with Dr. Abel in "Hannah & Her Sisters".

"They say that dames are simple. I never met one that didn't understand a slap in the mouth or a slug from a 45"
— Humphrey Bogart's advice to Woody in "Play It Again Sam"

WILLIS, GORDON

Famous cinematographer whose work for Allen includes "Annie Hall", "Interiors", "Zelig" and "Manhattan". Other notable achievements include "The Godfather Trilogy".

WING FAT

Shephard Wong's competitor searching for the secret egg salad recipe in "What's Up Tiger Lily?".

WOLF, FRANKIE (Micil Murphy)

Virgil's accomplice wanted by the Feds for dancing with a mailman in "Take The Money & Run"

WONG, SHEPHARD (Tadao Nakamaru)

Holds the egg salad recipe that will keep the The Grand Exhalted High Maka of Prosper off The Globe

YOKAHAMA HARBOR

Where Shephard Wong's gambling ship is moored.

YOLANDA (Natividad Abascal)

A well-endowed member of the rebel band in "Bananas"

*"If Christ were a carpenter, I
wonder what he charged for
bookshelves"*
*— Boris (Woody Allen) asks in
"Love & Death"*

YOU MAY BE SIX PEOPLE, BUT I LOVE YOU"

Sung by Bernie Knee, Steve Clayton, Tony Wells in "Zelig"

YOUNG GREGOR

The oldest of the Gregors in "Love & Death"

ZELIG, JACK

Leonard's brother, who has a nervous breakdown

ZELIG, LEONARD (Woody Allen)

Unable to fit in and still reeling from not having read "Moby Dick", Leonard adapts a personality where he literally metamorphosizes into the people he's with to fit in comfortably with them until Eudora Fletcher cures him in "Zelig"

ZELIG, LOU

Listed on roster of New York Yankees training Camp in Florida until he is discovered to be Leonard Zelig, the changing man.

ZELIG, MORRIS

Zelig's father, a Yiddish actor, played Puck in the Orthodox version of "Midsummer Night's Dream".

ZELIG, RUTH

Sister of Zelig, shoplifter and alcoholic who ultimately exploits Zelig as a moneymaking tool.

ZELMAN, LEONARD

aka Zelig

ZIPSKY, MR.

Runs down street brandishing meet cleaver in "Radio Days" in a fit of insanity.